FOUNDERS
&
FOLLOWERS

―――――――

Literary Lectures
given on the occasion of the
150th Anniversary
of the founding of
The London Library

SINCLAIR-STEVENSON

First published in Great Britain
by Sinclair-Stevenson
7/8 Kendrick Mews
London sw7 3HG England

A CIP catalogue record for this book
is available from the British Library.
ISBN 1 85619 171 0

Typeset by Rowland Phototypesetting Limited
Bury St Edmunds, Suffolk

Printed and bound in Great Britain
by St Edmundsbury Press Limited
Bury St Edmunds, Suffolk

CONTENTS

LIST OF ILLUSTRATIONS

Thomas Carlyle, c.1832
  (Anonymous drawing in the London Library; probably a copy
  of a Samuel Laurence portrait)
Richard Monckton Milnes, drawing by George Richmond
  (Reproduced from an engraving in The London Library)
George Eliot, drawing by Samuel Laurence, 1857
  (Reproduced by courtesy of Girton College, Cambridge)
George Henry Lewes, drawing by Rudolph Lehmann
  (Reproduced by courtesy of the British Museum, Department
  of Prints and Drawings)
Rudyard Kipling, drawing by William Strang, ARA
  (Reproduced by courtesy of the National Portrait Gallery,
  London)
Harold Nicolson, drawing by William Rothenstein, 1930
  (Reproduced by courtesy of Mr Nigel Nicolson)
Rose Macaulay, drawing by H. M. G. Wilson
  (Reproduced by courtesy of Messrs Hodder and Stoughton)
Sir Charles Hagberg Wright, drawing by William Rothenstein
  (Portrait in The London Library; reproduced by permission)

PREFACE

THE YEAR 1991 was exceptionally eventful for The London Library. It witnessed the start of the extension of its St James's Square property on the north elevation; the introduction of a computer which will contain the whole of the catalogue eventually and will also record all book movements; and the launch of an appeal to fund these two exciting projects. All this might have taken place at any time, but it is especially appropriate that it coincided with the year when the library's 150th anniversary was celebrated.

Specifically to mark that anniversary the committee of the library, under the chairmanship then of John Grigg, decided on several ventures: the striking of a commemorative medallion by the Royal Mint for sale to members; the holding of a party for 2,500 members and guests in St James's Square, with the library's patron, Queen Elizabeth the Queen Mother, as guest of honour; the encouraging of John Wells to write a history of the library; and the giving of seven literary lectures by distinguished members.

The lectures were given on successive Mondays at 6.30 in the evening. On 7th October Noel Annan, with Sir Steven Runciman in the chair, spoke on Thomas Carlyle; on 14th October Anthony Quinton, with Sir Nicholas Henderson in the chair, spoke on Richard Monckton Milnes; on 21st October A. S. Byatt, with Bamber Gascoigne in the chair, spoke on George Eliot and George Henry Lewes; on 28th October John Julius Norwich, with John Grigg in the chair, spoke on Rudyard Kipling; on 4th November Kenneth Rose, with Philip Ziegler in the chair, spoke on Harold Nicolson; on 11th November A. N. Wilson, with Lord Bonham-Carter in the chair, spoke on Rose Macaulay; and on 18th November John Wells, with Douglas Matthews in the chair, spoke on Some Previous Librarians.

Apart from the last lecture the subjects were all prominent literary figures who, with one exception, had held office in the library, ranging from the founder and president, Thomas Carlyle, to a chairman and members of the committee. Whilst George Eliot was not an office holder, her close association with G. H. Lewes, a long-serving member of the committee, almost gives her honorary status. The speakers, too, were drawn from present and former office holders. Only A. N. Wilson has not served in an official position, but his long membership testifies to his devotion to the library. Finally, the chairmen for the lectures included one vice-president, two former committee chairmen, committee members and the present librarian.

The lectures were open to all members, and they were entitled to bring guests. The attendance ranged from 450 to 750, and it was the magnitude of these numbers that caused the library to use the Logan Hall in Bedford Way, the lecture hall of the Institute of Education of the University of London. This had enough seating capacity and admirable lecture hall facilities, although it was a pity that the library itself was unable to provide sufficient accommodation for the large numbers attending.

The standard of the lectures was superb throughout, as readers will see for themselves. Members and their guests enjoyed the social warmth of the occasion, and the series brought an appropriate and happy conclusion to the library's celebratory year.

Lewis Golden

December 1991   Chairman
The London Library

INTRODUCTION

WHEN I WAS invited to write this introduction to the 150th anniversary lectures, my first thought was that the Library needs no testimonial from anyone: its distinction and fame – of which the occasional references to it by writers in some of the most distinguished works of the imagination of our time are sufficient evidence – are such that there was nothing I could say, however sincere, however laudatory. It is easily the best private library in the civilised world, that is to say, anywhere – even the Boston Athenaeum does not approach it in either its holdings or the opportunities it gives for borrowing a number of books at a time – which has been of help to a very wide variety of writers – academic, imaginative (not that academics invariably lack imagination), authors of memoirs and in every kind of genre that, for the most part, is likely to survive our time. The gratitude that its members feel towards the Library is, and has, I suspect, always been, immense. But perhaps I might attempt to say something about my own feelings towards it, which – apart from those which I share with so many others – are of a special kind. I hope that this will not seem too immodest or too personal.

I became a member of the Library, I think, almost sixty years ago, when I first began teaching at Oxford, soon after my election to All Souls. At first I used it much as anyone else might, for books that I needed both for work and pleasure, and sometimes both; and I used it in part as a club where I could meet other members – it was, and I hope still is, an excellent venue for appointments between members of the intelligentsia (I hope this description will not be taken amiss), and indeed, intelligent and civilised people, who haunt the Catalogue Room of the Library. I knew that the Library had a particularly fine collection of Russian books, made, I believe, by the Librarian Dr Hagberg Wright, who was a Russian scholar, and made it one of the best Russian and Scandinavian collections in the United Kingdom. The collection of nineteenth-century Russian litera- ture is truly remarkable, and contains, among other, better- known works, a number of rare and fascinating books some of which are not to be found in the British Library or anywhere else in Britain. Stimulated by this vague impression – I have no idea how I came by it – I went to the Russian shelves and glanced casually at them. Apart from the works of the great classical writers – I read Russian freely and supposed that I should find something of interest there – my eye lit on an author called Aleksandr Gerzen (better known as Alexander Herzen) – of whom at that time I knew virtually nothing. I did know vaguely that he was some sort of bearded nineteenth-century Russian worthy, who wrote on social issues, and I assumed that he was a half-forgotten Russian publicist, of interest to students of nineteenth-century Russian social writings – at that time I was not interested in this – but otherwise someone rather like, let us say at best, Buckle (once well known, now seldom read), or perhaps Harriet Martineau or Herbert Spencer or Benjamin Kidd (who remembers him? – yet his books were very well known in the 1890s) – in short, a justly forgotten Victorian sage. However, curiosity drove me to take out a volume, just to glance at it – it was the first volume of Herzen's memoirs, translated into English as 'My Past and Thoughts'. I vaguely began read- ing it, leaning against a shelf, and the first five pages appeared to me so fascinating that I took the volume out. After that, I read the entire work. I thought, and still think, that it is the best autobiography, or perhaps volume of memoirs, in the nineteenth century – not excluding Goethe or John Stuart Mill or the Gon- courts or anyone else. To begin with, it is beautifully written; moreover, it is based on marvellous powers of observation – its vignettes both of persons and of events, and of the author's relationships, seem to me unique. It is moving, often extremely entertaining, and contains a great deal of original thought both about situations and above all political and social ideas, to which tribute has not even today been sufficiently paid, even in his country of birth where he is worshipped (this is partly based on a deliberate misinterpretation of his position by the recent Soviet regime – Herzen was ferociously anti-communist). I can only say that I found some of his ideas of a degree of depth and boldness not paralleled by other thinkers of the Victorian age. He lived a great part of his life in England, and his descriptions of Englishmen, of the lives and conduct of foreign refugees among them (the most brilliant – and amusing – piece, perhaps, is a description of a political trial of two Frenchmen at the Old Bailey, which nothing but a reading of those pages can begin to convey), are wonderful. In short, I was infatuated with his writing and personality, and indeed I still am.

As a result of reading Herzen, I began reading books by and about his friends: Turgenev, Bakunin, Belinsky, Nekrasov, and the young Dostoyevsky (certainly an acquaintance and an admiring one, but not much of a friend) and others of that singularly gifted generation of Russian prose writers. At that time I was contemplating a book on Karl Marx, which I had been commissioned to do by the (at that time, I think) President of the Library, the (ever so) Rt. Hon. H. A. L. Fisher, Warden of New College, where I taught. The book, intended for the Home University Library, of which Fisher and Gilbert Murray were the editors, had first been offered to Harold Laski, then to the present Lord Longford, and after that, I think, to three or four others, all of whom declined to undertake it, and as a desperate measure he suggested that I might do something on this topic, provided I kept in mind that the audience for which these books were intended were squash professionals. I began reading Karl Marx and Herzen more or less simultaneously. Karl Marx was very heavy going – but I accepted the commission because I thought that Marxism would be of growing importance, I wished I knew something of it, and if I did not write about it I knew I could not bring myself to read those often punishing pages. But Herzen, by comparison, and indeed all the Russians of that period, were a marvellous relief; and so, in some curious tandem fashion, I taught myself as well as I could what nineteenth-century political thought among early European socialists and Russian radicals had been. The result was that I became addicted for life to Russian radical ideas, as well as the rich literature in which such ideas were incorporated – novels, poetry and the like – the only way of circumventing the censorship which then, as in our day, forbade the publication of any but completely conformist social and political opinions.

Soon after the war, when I decided to abandon pure philosophy for reasons which I need not go into here, I began to write and lecture on these Russians. The rest of my life has been spent more or less in this region, investigating the various tributaries of that powerful river. I think that I can truthfully say that my membership of the London Library eventually determined the direction of my interest – indeed, in some sense it can be said to have formed me – so that after abandoning pure philosophy I knew what I wished to do. I cannot deny that my interest in the Russian Revolution – which is one of the two seminal events in the twentieth century which have shaped our lives – was of greater interest to me that it might have been to others, because as a boy of eight I was in Petrograd when it happened, and remember it quite vividly. Nevertheless, it is the London Library and its Russian shelves which determined a large part of the thoughts and writings, such as they are, of which I am the author. Consequently it is with deep personal gratitude that I wish to salute this marvellous Library, which has done so much to enlarge my own horizon and that of so many others – there is no library which commands so much devotion – and say how pleased and honoured I am by my lifelong association with it. I can only repeat that if all this seems too self-centred and autobiographical, I apologise for inflicting it on the reader.

The Library is to be congratulated on its excellent initiative in arranging so impressive a series of lectures. Although this introduction is written before the first lecture has been delivered, I can only say that the names of the lecturers are a guarantee of their quality. This concluding achievement in its anniversary year will be a fitting celebration of the founding of our great Library.

Isaiah Berlin

THOMAS CARLYLE

1795–1881

NOEL ANNAN

THOMAS CARLYLE

IN APRIL 1837 the coaches of the well-to-do filled the street outside Willis's Rooms. It was there that Almack's Balls were held to which any family aspiring to enter London society went. But on this occasion the *beau monde* had been urged by that indefatigable man about town Dicky Monckton Milnes, to come and hear a handsome, uncouth Scotsman, already aged forty-two, deliver the first of a series of lectures on German literature. Thomas Carlyle was known to have published an extraordinary three volume work on the French Revolution. He was also known to have a bee in his bonnet about the need to found a London library. So it was not odd that, when a public meeting was called to canvass support for the project, he was one of the speakers. At that meeting, as Carlyle contemptuously recalled, 'with a lord in the chair', he argued that a club was not a place in which to read serious books. Nor for that matter was the then stuffy reading room of the British Museum ideal. One must be able to borrow books and read them at home. In his peroration he said of his brain-child, 'I call it a church which every devout soul may enter, a church without quarrelling and no church rates' – at which point he was drowned in cheers and laughter and sat down. Two years later the London Library was founded and we are here this evening to honour him.

But when you ask: who is this man we are honouring? You find yourself faced with a row of paradoxes. Carlyle was the son of a rough Scots mason from Annandale, on the Scottish border where my own ancestors came from. He was born at Ecclefechan and went to the grammar school at Annan where he was bullied because his mother forbade him to return blow for blow. He hated Edinburgh University. He hated university life not, like Milton or Gibbon, because he was better educated than his teachers – after all Edinburgh was then the best university in the United Kingdom at the high tide of the Scottish enlightenment. He hated Edinburgh because the professors were urbane, he was homely; they were chilly, he was arduous; they were intellectuals, he had a religious temperament; they relied on reason, he on conscience. He grew up to despise the rich, the cultured, the polite and all social graces; and he had a hard struggle to gain a living. He lost his first love to another, and nearly lost Jane Welsh before he married her.

And yet paradoxically he came to enjoy being lionised by London society and he succumbed to the fascination of the formidable mid-Victorian London hostess Lady Ashburton. He would desert his wife for weeks on end to join this or that country house party if Harriet Ashburton were there, he disapproving of the idle life of the aristocracy, she admiring her 'dear old prophet' and liking, as some women do, the streak of cruelty in a man.

His personal life was also paradoxical. He was the evangelist of Victorian manliness. He praised the simple domestic virtues and was a paragon of conjugal fidelity. But the evidence is pretty conclusive that he was impotent: he could not get an erection on his wedding night and his wife laughed at him. Within weeks they were sleeping in separate rooms, both practised insomniacs. He was also 'gey ill to live with' and broke his wife on the wheel of his egotism. Jane Carlyle was a spirited woman whose letters prove she had literary gifts of high order. But she was witty, malicious and gave her husband a hard time. The editor of *The Times* once said to her, 'Do you know, Mrs Carlyle, you would be vastly more amiable if you were not so damnably clever?' As

4

Samuel Butler said, it was a good thing the Carlyles married each other, thus saving four people from being miserable instead of only two.

Coming from such a poor but indomitable Lowland Scots background Carlyle was on the side of the underdog. Or was he? He certainly saw through the lie of nineteenth-century parliamentary democracy. He preached that man owes a duty to brother man. He satirised the aristocratic land-owning class for their ignorance and idleness and their indifference to the wretchedness of the poor in the cities. He was the first to understand that the industrialists – Plugson he called them – were grinding to pieces the multiple relationships between master and man that existed in an agricultural community. Plugson had reduced those relationships to one – the cash nexus. That was why Friedrich Engels praised and translated him. That was why Dickens dedicated *Hard Times* to him. That was why Emerson chose him as a correspondent, and Sterling and Froude felt he had given them a faith to live by. That was why Huxley wrote that *Sartor Resartus* convinced him that 'A deep sense of religion was compatible with an extra absence of theology'.[1] That is why the early leaders of the Labour Party such as Keir Hardie spoke of their debt to him.

But the same man is notorious today for parading his contempt for reformers and niggers, for revelling in the mailed fist, for defending Governor Eyre who massacred blacks in an uprising in Jamaica. This is the man who praised Dr Francia the dictator of Paraguay for hanging or shooting anyone who opposed his puritanical regime. So stark is the difference between *Past & Present* (1843) and the *Latter Day Pamphlets* (1850) that G. M. Trevelyan declared there were two Carlyles and bewailed a good man gone wrong. We must remember he was a Romantic, born in the same year as Keats. But he is a very

[1] *Sartor Resartus* (1834) Chapter 9

5

peculiar Romantic. He hated Byron as an aristocrat and a rich man, who flouted the domestic virtues. 'Close thy Byron, open thy Goethe', he said! Nor did he have any use for Shelley. The perfectibility of man was for him a wicked heresy. He had been brought up as a Calvinist, and although he lost his faith in dogmatic Christianity, he detested atheists or anyone who scoffed at Christian belief. He quoted Goethe. 'Wer darf Ihn nennen?' 'Who dares to name God?' Carlyle praised reverence, he believed that life is stern,

> 'Not a May game is this man's life; but
> a battle and a march, a warfare with
> principalities and powers. No idle
> promenade through fragrant groves and
> green flowery spaces, waited on by the
> choral muses and the rosy hours: it is
> a stern pilgrimage through burning sandy
> solitudes, through regions of thick-ribbed
> ice'.[1]

He often uses religious language, and no wonder, for though he lost his faith, he experienced a kind of conversion: what he called 'My spiritual new-birth or baphometic fire-baptism'.[2] He had been sunk in despair, appalled by the horrors of the world in which he lived. Suddenly he realised that one must say yes to life, not no. He came to see that 'the universe is not dead, and demoniacal, a charnel house with spectres; but God-like and my Father's'.

But do not be deceived by the religious language. Carlyle did not believe Christ was God. He thought immortality uncertain and a physical hell ridiculous. When Carlyle praised the gospel of work he did not mean that hard work cures egoism, cafard,

[1] *Past & Present* (1843) Book 4
[2] *Sartor Resartus* (1834) Chapter 7

anomie – what Kipling called 'The cameelious hump'. He meant that you have to annihilate the self in order to be born again.

Indeed, although Carlyle hated Byron, there is a lot of Byronism in him. The central fact of Byron's life was the exercise of the will and defiance in the face of good form society. Carlyle introduced the will as *the* great concept in his vision of history. He also rejected the rationalist, the positivist, theory of knowledge. Truth is not discovered by logical reasoning, it does not mount at compound interest as more scientific discoveries are made. On the contrary, truth cannot be pinned down, it is always changing. Carlyle prefigures Freud. He understands how the unconscious works in men – he wrote an essay on the 'Involuntary Unconscious'. Hidden in men's minds is a dynamo of crude energy. Thwart it at your peril. Carlyle saw this energy at work on the day that Louis XVI was forced by the mob to come to Paris. 'For they lie always, those subterranean Eumenides (fabulous and yet so true) in the dullest existence of man – and can dance, brandishing their dusky torches, shaking their serpent hair.'[1]

Carlyle was no schizophrenic. He was carved from a single block of granite, and if we are to understand why he became the strangest and most influential sage of his time, we must look at his profession. He was an historian, and an historian of startling originality and imagination who went dead against the accepted versions of history current at the time when the London Library was founded. In those lectures with which he made his name Carlyle gave an explanation of culture and of the way it develops through the great men who get others to accept that they should rule them. He also argued that the Christian culture that people took for granted was now at the end of its days. Yet if you asked philosophers what system of thought was going to replace

[1] *The French Revolution I* (1837) Book 7

7

Christianity, you would get a worthless answer. What answer did Carlyle give? The answer he gave was this.

The first culture Carlyle examined in his lectures was paganism. He at once attacked the bias of his contemporaries who regarded pagan gods as ridiculous. The worship of Odin was not to be dismissed as erroneous idolatry, since it recognised the divine quality of nature and esteemed valour which was the fountain of all pity and truth. At its best it was a religion of 'transcendent wonder', a quality totally lacking in the modern world which would not worship a man such as Luther but merely 'took the dimensions of him'. Scandinavian sincerity was superior to Greek gracefulness of expression. True, the Greeks had produced a hero, the much-enduring Odysseus, but 'there is no word of life in Socrates': indeed the Greek genius 'displays itself with as curious a felicity as the French does in frivolous exercises'. Thrift and discipline enabled the Romans to surpass the Greeks though in the end they were corrupted by the Greek mania for speculation. Mahomet was a hero: whether he spoke the truth was irrelevant, since it was quackery to imagine that religion could be proved. A false man could not have founded a religion, and his earnestness kindled the world. He spoke seldom but his speech was meaningful, and hence the Syrian Christians collapsed before him, still arguing about the iota – whether the relations between the Father and the Son within the Godhead should be expressed as homoousion or homoiousion. Nor should we denigrate the Middle Ages, a time when men were loyal to their superiors and the church enforced emperors to acknowledge that spiritual life was all-important. Medieval men were 'in contact with fact and reality' and Christianity inherited from stoicism the doctrine of 'belief in one's self'. Carlyle singled out the Swiss, the Dutch and the Moors for praise but awarded the palm to the teutonic qualities of the Germans who had bequeathed us trial by jury; and since Saxons and Normans were both teutonic, Englishmen, too, exhibited an energy which was shown

8

in work not words. Luther was to be preferred to Erasmus, for Luther perceived that men were being taught to worship a symbol of God not God himself. Dante and Shakespeare were poet heroes, poetry being musical thought. John Knox was also a hero. He gave Scotland its soul – a soul being different from the Glorious Revolution of 1688 and habeas corpus.

Carlyle loathed the eighteenth century as an era lacking sincerity and governed by quackery. But he allowed it had its heroes – Johnson, a man who discovered that originality did not mean novelty. He even allowed greatness to Voltaire and Rousseau 'a sadly contracted hero' or Bentham who was filled with 'eyeless heroism' – he allowed them greatness because all three were in earnest. But he pointed the moral by contrasting them with Cromwell and Napoleon because both gave men a centre to revolve around after a revolution. Cromwell was superior because he had the great English talent for silence. He thought facts more important than constitutions.

Such was Carlyle's account of the past. The revulsion today from narrative history and the fashion of analysing social movements and the impersonal forces that shape society make it sound like a fifteen-year-old schoolboy's first attempt at writing a history essay. And yet the equal passion of our times for biography shows that we have not totally discarded Carlyle's view that history is at any rate in part about people. He sets his characters before a vast proscenium arch on the amphitheatre of time, there to play out the drama of the destiny of man. Not for him the hesitations and balancing of possibilities that scholars such as Dryasdust engage in. Not for him the reconstruction and the impact of social controls upon classes and groups. His history rises on the wings of his style. And his style is the most individual and peculiar of any British historian. It is a style that transformed English prose. It destroyed Johnsonian English. Dickens and dozens of other writers learned from Carlyle to break out of grammatical rules and write sentences without verbs. His style is grotesque, sardonic, inventive, capable at once of suggesting a set of values different from those of his reader yet relentlessly pressing upon him facts which he has to recognise as valid for his own times as for the past.

He invents words. He was struck by the reply of a witness in a trial under cross-examination.

– What sort of person was Mr Weare?
– He was always a respectable person.
– What do you mean by respectable?
– He kept a gig.

So Carlyle coined the word gig-men or gigmantity as a term of opprobrium. Here are some of the last sentences of the *French Revolution*:

'Respectability with all her collected Gigs inflamed for funeral pyre, wailing leaves, the Earth; not to return save under new Avatar. The world is black ashes . . . all dwellings of men destroyed; the very mountains peeled and riven, the valleys black and dead: it is an empty world! . . . For it is the end of the Dominion of *Imposture* (Which is Darkness and opaque fire-damp); and the burning up with unquenchable fire of all the Gigs that are in the Earth, . . .'[1]

The object of his style is to work on the imagination of the reader and compel him to assent in an emotion of wonder and pity. He reports like a journalist – but, no, the simile is inappropriate – he leads like Dante's Virgil his reader through the hell and purgatory of human endeavour. He will seize on a minor personality or event and make it significant. He never sentimentalises the past but he broods on the irony of man's existence. Writing of the battlefield of Naseby he recollects how a friend of his had

[1] *The French Revolution III* (1837) Book 7

a couple of molar teeth in his cabinet dug up from the battlefield which had eaten their breakfast on the morning of the 14th of June and, clenched in battle, had never any more work to do in this world.

Carlyle communicates as few others have done the historian's emotion at discovering the past and his frustration when his sources dry up on him.

Those clear eyes of neighbour Jocelin looked on the bodily presence of King John; the very John *Sansterre*, or Lackland, who signed the *Magna Charta* afterwards in Runnymead. Lackland, with a great retinue, boarded once, for the matter of a fortnight, in St Edmundsbury Convent; daily in the very eyesight, palpable to the very fingers of our Jocelin: O Jocelin, what did he say, what did he do: how looked he, lived he; – at the very lowest what coat or breeches had he on? Jocelin is obstinately silent. Jocelin marks down what interests *him*; entirely deaf to us. With Jocelin's eyes we discern almost nothing of John Lackland. As through a glass darkly, we with our own eyes and appliances, intensely looking, discern at most: a blustering, dissipated human figure, with a kind of blackguard quality air, in cramoisy, velvet, or other uncertain texture, uncertain cut, with much plumage and fringing; amid numerous other human figures of the like; riding abroad with hawks; talking noisy nonsense; – tearing out the bowels of St Edmundsbury Convent (its larders namely and cellars) in the most ruinous way, by living at rack and manger there. Jocelin notes only, with a slight subacidity of manner, that the King's majesty *Dominus Rex*, did leave, as gift for our St Edmund shrine, a handsome enough silk cloak, – or rather pretended to leave, for one of his retinue borrowed it of us, and we never got sight of it again; and on the whole, that the *Dominus Rex*, at departing, gave us 'thirteen *Sterlingii*' one shilling and one

11

penny, to say a mass for him; and so departed, – like a
shabby Lackland as he was! 'Thirteen pence sterling', this
was what the Convent got from Lackland, for all the vic-
tuals he and his had made away with. We of course said
our mass for him, having covenanted to do it, – but let
impartial prosterity judge with what degree of fervour!

And in this manner vanishes King Lackland.[1]

But Carlyle's originality as a historian was most striking when
we consider how he treated the French Revolution. For Englishmen, when Victoria came to the throne, the last word on that
event had been said by Burke. But Carlyle saw nothing to admire
to the eighteenth-century civilisation which Burke defended
against the Jacobins.

To me the eighteenth century has nothing grand in it,
except that grand universal suicide, named French Revolution, by which it terminated its otherwise most worthless
existence with at least one worthy act; setting fire to its
old home and self; and going up in flames and volcanic
explosions, in a truly memorable and important manner. A
very fit termination, as I thankfully feel, for such a century.
Century spendthrift, fraudulent – bankrupt; gone at length
utterly insolvent, without real *money* of performance in its
pocket, and the shops declining to take hypocrisies and
speciosities any farther: – what could the poor century do,
but at length admit, 'Well, it is so. I am a swindler-century,
and have long been; having learned the trick of it from my
father and grandfather; knowing hardly any trade but that
in false bills, which I thought foolishly might last forever,
and still bring at least beef and pudding to the favoured of
mankind. And behold it ends; and I am a detected swindler,
and have nothing even to eat. What remains but that I

---

[1] *Past & Present* (1843) Book 2

blow my brains out, and do at length one true action?'
Which the poor century did; many thanks to it, in the
circumstances.[1]

Carlyle did not praise the French Revolution as Tom Paine did
for establishing the rights of man. For Carlyle the Revolution
was a judgement on the French or on Dubarrydom as he called
it – a judgement the English had the luck to escape because they
had not been corrupted by the Jesuits. What happens when a
nation is irretrievably corrupted? How can it renew itself? Carlyle believed that in many cases only through revolutionary force
could a new order be born. He dismissed the liberal constitution-
alism of the Girondins as simply the imposition of rule by the
middle class. He was unique in not condemning the terror. In
one of his memorable metaphors Carlyle declared that without
sans-culottism the old clothes of the Ancien Regime could never
have been shed. His passage on the execution of Robespierre is
remarkable for its compassion towards the author and defender
of the Terror.

> Robespierre lay in an anteroom of the Convention hall,
> while his prison-escort was getting ready; the mangled jaw
> bound up rudely with bloody linen: a spectacle to men. He
> lies stretched on a table, a deal-box his pillow; the sheath
> of the pistol is still clenched convulsively in his hand. Men
> bully him, insult him: his eyes still indicate intelligence; he
> speaks no word. He had on the sky-blue coat he had got
> made for the 'Feast of the *Etre Suprême*' – O reader, can thy
> hard heart hold out against that? His trousers were nan-
> keen; the stockings had fallen down over the ankles. He
> spake no word more in this world.
>
> At the foot of the scaffold, they stretched him on the
> ground till his turn came. Lifted aloft, his eyes again

[1] *History of Friedrich II of Prussia, called 'Frederick the Great'* (1865) Book I

13

opened; caught the bloody axe. Samson wrenched the coat off him; wrenched the dirty linen from his jaw: the jaw fell powerless, there burst from him a cry; – hideous to hear and see. Samson, thou canst not be too quick!

Samson's work done, there bursts forth shout on shout of applause. Shout, which prolongs itself not only over Paris, but over France, but over Europe, and down to this generation. Deservedly, and also undeservedly. O unhappiest advocate of Arras, wert thou worse than other advocates? Stricter man, according to his formula, to his credo and his cant, of probities, benevolences, pleasures-of-virtue, and such like, lived not in that age. A man fitted, in some luckier settled age, to have become one of those incorruptible barren pattern-figures, and have had marble-tablets and funeral-sermons. His poor landlord, the cabinet-maker in the Rue Saint-Honoré, loved him; his brother died for him. May God be merciful to him, and to us![1]

One American scholar was so impressed by Carlyle's defence of Sans-culottism that he argued Carlyle almost prefigured Chairman Mao in maintaining that the organic growth of society can occur only in an atmosphere of revolutionary activism – of communal action by working class groups through society.[2] I do not think this can be sustained. Carlyle considered that institutionalised anarchy was a contradiction in terms. But Carlyle understood the problem. How can those vital forces that renew society find leadership? He answered: certainly not through despicable parliamentary government. Certainly not as the radicals and Bentham's followers believed through the scientific study of society. Wherever great things get debated in terms of logic, Carlyle said, 'they are as good as lost. Logic pretends to enforce

---

[1] *The French Revolution III* (1837) Book 6
[2] Philip Rosenberg *The Seventh Hero: Thomas Carlyle and the Theory of Radical Activism* (1974)

men to adopt a belief, and yet there is no constraint possible that way'. Accept rationalism and the sociological explanation of events, and history is depersonalised. Nor will Christianity help. Men are indeed the slaves of necessity, driven like sheep by the pressure of events which they can't control. Christians claim that God's providence breaks the chain of necessity and history is the working out of God's purpose. But Carlyle cannot believe in miracles and direct interference by God in the affairs of the world. It is not God who intervenes in human affairs but man. Society is always changing. There are cycles of growth and decay but they do not occur in a fixed order. They occur because man changes history. Nor is this surprising because man is the living organism within society. But only an exceptional man can change it. That man we call a hero.

The hero is a man who recognises the facts. Most men won't recognise them. Carlyle's facts are what today we would call necessity. The hero seizes on the facts and bends them to his will. He can't alter them, but he can, as it were, leap on to the back of history and ride it towards a goal of his own choice. By recognising necessity he becomes free.

This conception of history is not absurd. Men cannot hold back the tide of the impersonal forces in history, the changes in climate, trade, population etc. But their leaders can change the course the tide takes. Who can doubt that Hitler and Stalin changed its course in our time? Carlyle went on to say that the hero can do this only if he *believes* in some great ideal or religion. He can't do it if he *debates* matters. He chooses his destination by intuition not by logic. Belief enables him to act and action preserves the life-force in society – what Carlyle calls the Tree of Isdragil, the symbol of growth, of progress.

Well, you may ask, belief in what? Carlyle is anything but precise. Belief in the saved, belief in the devil, belief in the difference between right and wrong. Recognition that man is a poor thing, slothful, timorous, mean in spirit – that is why

15

schemes for universal brotherhood and perpetual peace are so dangerous. Believe in those and you will be destroyed by mob rule, by Sans-culottism. For while it is true that Carlyle thought the French eighteenth century was bound to be destroyed by violence, he hated the ideas that sustained the French Revolution, and he hated mob-rule. Why his history of the Revolution is a masterpiece is because he makes intelligible the relations between the impersonal forces of historical necessity and the men and women of those times in whose grasp they struggle. The Revolution had unleashed wicked passions and false views of life, and we would have to wait, he said 'two centuries, hardly less, before democracy goes through its due stage of quackocracy; and a pestilential world would be burnt up and have begun to grow green and young again'.[1]

Out of all the heroes Carlyle mentioned in the series of lectures he gave in 1840, he chose two on which to write at length – Cromwell and Frederick the Great. Cromwell is perhaps too much a threnody over the old Puritan tradition. The analysis of Frederick the Great is very different and is often condemned as a failure. Carlyle is said to have mistaken a card-sharper for a hero and to have indulged his spleen against parliamentary democracy by justifying power politics and maintaining that might is right. But such a judgement overlooks the fact that Carlyle was wrestling with a real problem. How is it possible for a statesman of a second-rate indigent power, who is in duty bound to further his country's interests, to accomplish his ends without resorting to trickery and treachery to his enemies and allies? What moral standards in reality obtain in international usage? Liberal statesmen and philosophers disliked answering these questions for they were accustomed to think in terms of freedom not of power. Carlyle relished their discomfiture. Moreover, he played a trick on those who thought they understood

---

[1] *The French Revolution III* (1837) Book 6

the concept of the hero. Carlyle deliberately showed Frederick to be little more than normal size because he wanted to emphasise that all human beings must learn that their powers are limited and that brute force alone is unavailing: the hero must be instinctively cunning, and twist, rather than overcome, fate. Frederick's genius lay in conquering the false spirit of his own century and in realising that man can hold that which he gains only by resourcefulness, not through dreams of universal peace and brotherhood; and Carlyle sets against Frederick in his drama the figure of Voltaire.

Voltaire too was adroit, and Carlyle praises him. 'The beagles of the hierarchy and the monarchy, proverbially quick of scent and sharp of tooth, are out in quest of him; but this is a lion-fox which cannot be captured.' 'He can raise no standing armies for his defence; yet he too is a European power and not undefended: an invisible impregnable bulwark, – that of public opinion, defends him. Few private men have had so wide a circle of charity and have watched over it so well.' What defect then denies Voltaire the full title of hero? It is 'his entire want of earnestness'. He is a mocker, a master of ridicule. But ridicule is a small faculty. Voltaire is inspired by denial, the everlasting nay. 'Reverence, the highest feeling that man's nature is capable of, the crown of his whole moral manhood . . . he seems not to understand.' His theory of the world is little, a picture of self, and he reads history simply through a pair of anti-Catholic spectacles.

On the other hand Frederick is taught by his brutal father to face reality. His father killed the eighteenth-century spirit in him, when he condemned the young Frederick to watch his great friend Katte being executed because he and Katte had been revolted by the King's Prussian brutality. Carlyle, as he grew older, revelled in the harshness of the decisions the hero has to take. Frederick's equivocations and brutal decisions are to be condoned as the hero's understanding of his destiny.

Those of us who lived through the thirties well remember this frame of mind. We remember Auden's line in his poem on Spain – a line he afterwards repudiated with horror – 'The conscious guilt in the necessary murder'. We may remember the veteran communist Victor Kiernan recalling how the young John Cornford told him with relish how Bela Kun machine-gunned 5,000 prisoners as an act of policial necessity. The communists in the thirties excused themselves by arguing that the alternative to the necessary murder was too terrible to contemplate – the triumph of fascism: and in this war against evil, man must accept that eggs may have to be broken in order that the perfect omelette be cooked.

Carlyle too had his excuse. It was not for nothing that he had been brought up a Calvinist. The Calvinist believes that men and women are divided into the small band of the elect and the vast majority who will suffer in hell throughout eternity for their sins because God has not elected them to be saved. Nothing you do on your own can affect the outcome. You gain grace and glory only if God has given you the gift of final perseverance. This is the necessary end of mankind, and inescapable necessity. So in Carlyle man saves himself not through arguing against the course of history but accepting it. He accepts the inevitability of historical necessity which a hero cannot reverse but may turn to his advantage. It is interesting that from time to time intelligent and serious men find this vision of life not merely acceptable but enjoyable. Who reads the Thirty-nine articles of the Church of England these days? But if you do you will find that the seventeenth article refers to the Doctrine of Predestination which, it says, is of 'sweet, pleasant and unspeakable comfort'. To believe as Calvinists do, and as communists used to do, that they were of the elect, superior to their contemporaries, is a delectable state of mind.

Carlyle used to be written off as a proto-Nazi during the Second World War. From this fate he was rescued by a young British scholar who was to make his home in America. Eric

Bentley was the first to place Carlyle's theory of heroes in its historical perspective and trace the notion of the Superman as it evolved from Carlyle through Nietzsche and Wagner through Shaw to D. H. Lawrence.[1] His study remains the best account of Carlyle's place in the history of ideas; and Carlyle takes his place among those German and Russian Romantic thinkers about whom Isaiah Berlin has written with such illumination – men who found the rationalist or the empirical interpretation of knowledge and culture inadequate and misleading. Anyone who wants to discover the antecedents of Carlyle's ideas and his style should soak himself in the writings of the German Romantic, Jean Paul Richter, an experience few will be willing to endure.

As for Carlyle's disciples – they must appear today few on the ground. And yet there is one who dominated Britain in the eighties. Margaret Thatcher is a notable disciple of Carlyle's doctrine of work. She too was dissatisfied with the polite version of politics. She too preferred to emphasise the vigorous virtues rather than the softer virtues of humility, gentleness, sympathy and kindness. She enjoyed making a robust response to critics and disbelievers.

All the same, few today find that grim, sardonic Scotsman an attractive figure; and perhaps you need a touch of Scots blood to appreciate the particular art of his put-down of people. He was not kind about his contemporaries. Of Lamb he said, 'A more pitiful, rickety, grasping, staggering, stammering Tom Fool I do not know'. Keble was a little ape, Newman had the intellect of a good sized rabbit, Gladstone was 'a spectral kind of phantasm of a man – nothing in him but form and ceremonies and outsize wrappings'. As for Disraeli, he was a 'cursed old Jew not worth his weight in bacon'. But in his considered writings Carlyle left marvellous portraits of individuals. Here he is on Coleridge in old age:

[1] Eric Bentley *The Cult of the Superman* (1947)

To sit as a passive bucket and be pumped into, whether you consent or not, can in the long-run be exhilarating to no creature; how eloquent-soever the flood of utterance that is descending. But if it be withal a confused unintelligible flood of utterance, threatening to submerge all known landmarks of thought, and drown the world and you! – I have heard Coleridge talk, with eager musical energy, two stricken hours, his face radiant and moist, and communicate no meaning whatsoever to any individual of his hearers, – certain of whom, I for one, still kept eagerly listening in hope; the most had long before given up, and formed (if the room were large enough) secondary humming groups of their own. He began anywhere: you put some question to him, made some suggestive observation: instead of answering this, or decidedly setting out towards answer of it, he would accumulate formidable apparatus, logical swim-bladders, transcendental life-preservers and other precautionary and vehiculatory gear, for setting out: perhaps did at last get under way, – but was swiftly solicited, turned aside by the glance of some radiant new game on this hand or that, into new courses; and ever into new; and before long into all the universe, where it was uncertain what game you would catch, or whether any.

He had knowledge about many things and topics, much curious reading; but generally all topics led him, after a pass or two, into the high seas of theosophic philosophy, the hazy infinitude of Kantean transcendentalism, with its 'Sum-m-njects' and 'Om-m-mjects'.

Glorious islets, too, I have seen rise out of the haze; but they were few, and soon swallowed in the general element again. Balmy, sunny islets, islets of the blest and the intelligible: – on which occasions those secondary humming groups would all cease humming, and hang breathless upon the eloquent words; till once your islet got wrapt in the mist again, and they could recommence humming. Eloquent artistically expressive words you always had; piercing radiances of a most subtle insight came at intervals; tones of noble pious sympathy, recognizable as pious though strangely coloured, were never wanting long: but in general you could not call this aimless, cloudcapt, cloud-based, lawlessly meandering human discourse of reason by the name of 'excellent talk', but only of 'surprising'; and were reminded bitterly of Hazlitt's account of it: 'excellent talker, very, – if you let him start from no premises and come to no conclusion.'[1]

Carlyle was indeed a master of an art now practically extinct among historians. He was a master of description, and by description rendering an incident, an event, in the past memorable. In *Recreations of an Historian* he considered how this was done:

Often a slight circumstance contributes curiously to the result; a light-gleam, which instantaneously *excites* the mind, and urges it to complete the picture, and evolve the meaning thereof for itself. But the power to select such features as will produce them, is generally treated by critics as a knack, or trick of the trade, a secret for being 'graphic'; whereas these magical feats are, in truth, rather inspirations; and the gift of performing them, which acts unconsciously, without forethought, is properly a *genius* for description.

That was the technique. But what was the secret of the power that he knew was in him?

One grand, invaluable secret there is, however, which includes all the rest: *to have an open loving heart, and what*

---

[1] *Life of John Sterling* (1851)

follows from the possession of such. This it is that opens the whole mind, quickens every faculty of the intellect to do its fit work, that of *knowing*: and therefrom, by sure consequence, of *vividly uttering-forth.* Other secret for being 'graphic' is there none, worth having: but this is an all-sufficient one. See, for example, what a small Boswell can do! Hereby, indeed, is the whole man made a living mirror, wherein the wonders of this ever-wonderful universe are, in their true light (which is ever a magical, miraculous one), represented, and reflected back on us. 'The heart sees farther than the head.'[1]

What are we to make of him? Let George Eliot help us. She said:

You may meet a man whose wisdom seems unimpeachable, since you find him in entire agreement with yourself; but this oracular man of unexceptionable opinions becomes a bore: while another man who deals in what you cannot but think dangerous paradoxes warms your heart by the pressure of his hand and looks out upon the world with so clear and loving an eye that nature seems to reflect the light of his glance upon your own feeling. So it is with Carlyle.[2]

Thomas Carlyle did not show much heart to the men and women he knew personally. But his heart went out to those whom he did not know, to the poor who slaved in factories, and to the dead who had lived and suffered in days long ago.

[1] 'Biography', quoted in *Recreations of an Historian* (1839)
[2] George Eliot *Essays and Leaves from a Note-Book* (1884)

RICHARD
MONCKTON MILNES

1809–1885

———————————————

ANTHONY QUINTON

RICHARD
MONCKTON MILNES

THE TOWN OF CREWE, in the north-west of England, is not, I understand, a place of very marked intrinsic charm or beauty. The Michelin Guide refers, rather furtively, to a Market Hall. Murray's Blue Guide speaks only of its role in modern industrial history as the home of a railway carriage works and as a major railway junction, connecting lines from Liverpool, Manchester, Chester and other more interesting spots. I speak largely on authority in this matter since although, like many others, I have passed through it and even changed trains at it, I have not left the station to have a look around.

What connects it to Richard Monckton Milnes is, in the first place, the fact of his marriage to The Hon. Annabelle Crewe. Her brother, the absurdly named, and absurd, Hungerford Crewe, who lived at Crewe Hall, had no children. His title passed to Robert, the only son of Annabelle and Richard Monckton Milnes, who raised himself to the rank of Marquess of Crewe by various forms of conspicuous public service. So the genealogical identity of Richard Monckton Milnes came to be obliterated in the ancient glory of his wife's background, as elevated to greater prominence by the efforts of his son.

But there is a certain appropriateness in the absorption of Monckton Milnes into Crewe. Like the town he is less important in himself than in his connections. He knew everybody: Tennyson, Gladstone, Peel, Palmerston, Thackeray, King Louis Philippe, the Emperor Napoleon III, Guizot, Thiers, Tocqueville,

25

Lamennais, Montalembert, Emerson, Whitman, Henry Adams and Henry James – to take at random a few of the people whom he had not simply met and talked to, but got to know well. He was held in deep affection by two notoriously difficult men: Landor and Carlyle. He helped to rescue Keats from the abyss of neglect and remote disapproval into which he had fallen soon after his death. He did much to assist and generally bring on Swinburne, although in the course of doing so he helped to fuel Swinburne's obsession with the Marquis de Sade by supplying the poet with Sade's works from his large pornographic collection. He took a great deal of trouble to get Coventry Patmore a job when Patmore was in a very distressed state. He was also like Crewe in being nothing much to look at.

So far as history is concerned he lives only through the others whom he helped, entertained at his breakfasts or in the country, charmed and amused. His direct achievements have altogether faded from view. He represented Pontefract in the House of Commons from 1837, entering Parliament at the age of twenty-eight in the election following the new Queen's accession to the throne, to 1863, when Palmerston had him made Lord Houghton as a modest aspect of the celebrations attending the marriage of the Prince of Wales to Alexandra of Denmark. Despite creditably regular attendance in Parliament, given his love of travel and the enormous inroads of his social calendar, and his persistent appeals to the succession of prime ministers to whom he attached himself – Peel and Palmerston in particular – he never achieved office. He thought himself qualified, by the unparalleled width of his acquaintances in and his knowledge of the capitals of Europe, to be foreign secretary. But the thought of such an appointment does not seem to have entered the heads of those who were in a position to bring it about. He was seen, surely with justice, as altogether too lightweight a figure. Disraeli, one of the very few people who actively disliked him, said that he was unique, not merely in the badness of his first speech in Parliament (something Disraeli knew about from personal experience), but in the fact that his subsequent speeches got progressively worse.

Nor did he do better in literature, his other favourite field. In early life he wrote about his travels, especially in Greece and further east. But *Memorials of a Tour in some parts of Greece: Chiefly Poetical* was wholly extinguished by the *Eothen* of his friend Kinglake and the almost equally successful *The Crescent and the Cross* of his friend Warburton. He published a number of volumes of verse: *Poems of Many Years* (which came out when he was twenty-nine), *Poems Legendary and Historical* and *Poetry for the People*. But they did not amount to much. He is represented by only one poem in Quiller-Couch's *Oxford Book of English Verse*, a collection notorious for its piety towards the more boneless kind of nineteenth-century composition. From later, similarly standard collections he has been altogether excluded.

His special gifts as an unusual social being developed soon after he established himself at the age of twenty-eight in London in rooms above 26 Pall Mall. These were, until his marriage, fourteen years later, the scene of his famous breakfast parties, where every kind of lion, actual or potential, political or literary, friendly or hostile, was brought together. It was soon after his inauguration in London as a new MP and all-encompassing host that he first met Thomas Carlyle. So when, a few years later, Carlyle was casting about for help with the London Library he was projecting, it was natural enough that he should rope in his new young friend, the breadth of whose acquaintance was already unrivalled and who was blessed with a willingness to follow through in practice the missions he had undertaken. The idea of a really serious subscription library in London would no more have occurred to him than any other idea. But once it had been formulated no-one was better equipped to help in its realisation.

27

Richard Monckton Milnes's origins were comparatively modest on his father's side. His grandfather was a well-off manufacturer from Wakefield, a Whig and a non-conformist M.P. for York. For fourteen years after 1784 he helped Fox with financial support. It was he who bought Fryston Hall which Richard Monckton Milnes eventually inherited. The latter's handsome father, a true horseman and lover of rural pleasures, came into possession of Fryston at the age of twenty-one on *his* father's death. Soon afterwards he entered the House of Commons for Pontefract, the seat his son Richard was eventually to take over from him. In 1808 he married the daughter of Lord Galway, and in the following year his only son Richard was born. A daughter, Harriet, who turned out to be taller and better-looking than her brother, followed in due course. Richard was brought up in the fairly modest house near Doncaster his father had rented and was taught at home by a tutor because of his delicate health. Richard's father was in somewhat reduced circumstances because of the family's debts of his brother. This was to have an important and not disagreeable effect on Richard. If it meant that he was brought up in a less grand house than he might have been, it also introduced him early in life to the charms of European travel when his parents moved to Milan in 1828. They stayed out of England until Robert Milnes's finances had been brought back into a sufficient state of repair in 1835, after nearly eight years away.

Richard arrived in Cambridge, as an undergraduate at Trinity, at the age of eighteen in 1827, shortly before his family's emigration. It was an auspicious moment for anyone with his taste for interesting company. He soon became friendly with Arthur Hallam and with the members of his circle: Tennyson above all, but also Kinglake, of *Eothen*, Spedding, the industrious editor of Bacon, and Dean Merivale. Thackeray and Edward Fitzgerald were at Cambridge at the time but he did not get to know them until later. He was to go to a public execution in

1840 with Thackeray, which he seems to have found a good deal
less upsetting than Thackeray did.

The appearance in Milnes's story of Hallam and Tennyson
provides an opportunity for a brief inspection of his poetical
gifts. Like Tennyson he was much upset by Hallam's death,
although not quite so much. Certainly his own lines on the
matter are in fairly stark contrast to *In Memoriam.*

I'm not where I was yesterday
Though my home be still the same,
For I have lost the veriest friend
Whom ever a friend could name;
I'm not where I was yesterday,
Though change there be little to see,
For a part of myself has lapsed away
From Time to Eternity.

Various defects conspire to mar this expression of entirely sincere regret: its inappropriately cheerful cantering *John Gilpin*-like
metre; the clumsy departures from it (though *change* there be
little to *see*); the faded, conventional vocabulary ('veriest', 'lapsed
away'). He was active in both the Union and the Apostles, which
had been founded as the Conversazione Society a few years
before in 1820. It was as a representative of the Union that he
travelled to Oxford in 1829, with Hallam, to defend the claims
of Shelley against Byron at the corresponding institution there.
The main importance of the occasion for Milnes was his first
meeting with Gladstone, whom he described, without irony, as
'a very superior person'. Unlike many debaters, Hallam and
Milnes were sincerely attached to the poet they were defending.
In Hallam's circle there was a general reaction against Byron in
favour of the unfashionable Wordsworth and the still unestab-
lished Shelley and Keats. In retreat from Byronism and, indeed,
the haughty, cold-hearted form of masculinity of the Regency
period, Milnes's Cambridge friends were warmly affectionate,

decorated their conversation and correspondence with endearments and often broke into tears. It is possible to speculate on how far this all went. They do not seem to have had anything much of an amorous nature to do with women, on the commercial terms which were all that was available to them, in the manner of their eighteenth-century predecessors.

Milnes had fled in nervous despair from some examinations in Cambridge at the end of his second year and in April 1830 he left the place altogether. For a while he attended lectures at the newly opened University College, London. Later that year he joined the rest of his family in Milan, passing through Germany on the way and trying out his recently acquired grasp of the language. He developed a marked affection for Germany and things German which was not to be seriously diminished until Bismarck crushed France with what Milnes saw as exorbitant brutality forty-five years later. He acknowledged a considerable affinity to the place: 'the thing I was intended for by nature,' he said, 'is a German woman'. A little later he experienced a comparable enchantment on visiting Venice. The European exile of the Milneses was not total. Milnes was soon home for a visit to his great-aunt in London and then made a tour of grand houses in Ireland, observing, without any evident striving for effect, that Dublin was not up to Venice. Visiting Rome he met a host of notables, among them Wiseman, head of the English College and in time to return to England as cardinal. This meeting may have helped, along with Milnes's generally very liberal and religiously unenthusiastic attitude, to produce the calming good sense of his pamphlet *One Tract More* on the Oxford Movement a decade later. Wiseman does not reappear in Milnes's life, but others met in Rome do: Baron Bunsen, who was rather too austere fully to perceive the kind heart under Milnes's levity, and the French Catholic reformers Lammenais and Montalembert.

He soon went further afield, to Naples and Pompeii and then

to Greece, which was still in a chaotic state after its newly achieved independence. Despite his anti-Byronism he sought gossip about Byron. He felt indignant at what he described in his *Memorials* as the spoliation of the Parthenon by Lord Elgin. In 1837 he went down with malaria, which he had contracted in Florence, and made the first of his major conquests of difficult literary heroes. (His enduring friendship with Tennyson was established too early in the lives of both of them to count here, although its uninterrupted continuation is to the credit of both of them.)

Landor was living outside Florence in Fiesole at the time, keeping relatively quiet after a long series of explosive collisions. The reciprocal affection between the ancient, haughty, pugnacious, classically minded master of style in prose and poetry and the young, short, plump, curly-haired, paradox-emitting chatterbox is agreeable to contemplate. A few years later Landor was even heard to proclaim that 'Milnes is the greatest poet now living in England'.

In a pleasant essay of Milnes's on Landor, in his *Monographs Personal and Social* of 1873, two years before his own death, he wrote of him: 'under the most fortunate circumstances it is difficult to imagine Landor a comfortable Country Gentleman. For field sports, in which the unoccupied upper classes of this country expend harmlessly so much of the superfluous energy and occasional savagery of their dispositions, he had no taste. In his youth he had shot a partridge one winter afternoon, and found the bird alive the next morning, after a night of exceptional bitterness. "What that bird must have suffered," he exclaimed, "I often think of its look" – and he never took gun in hand again.' The more Boythorn-like side of Landor is recalled in the story of Landor throwing an Italian cook, whose dish had failed to please, out of the window and crying as the man crashed into the garden bed, 'Good God, I forgot the violets'.

Important for the future was Milnes's meeting, during his

31

weeks as Landor's guest, with Charles Brown, who had collected all the papers of and relating to Keats he could get hold of. Unable to publish a biography of Keats himself, he eventually handed them over to Milnes and his confidence was well placed. In 1848 Brown's memoir and other papers were the nucleus of Milnes's effective rescue of Keats from obscurity and disparagement in his *Life, Letters and Literary Remains of John Keats*, the most significant by far of his publications.

In 1835 the Milnes family returned to England. Fryston Hall, which Milnes did not like – it was in an ugly, industrially polluted neighbourhood and chaotically constructed – now became their headquarters. Milnes inherited it in the late 1850s. Turning his back on its surroundings and the unappealing activities that went on there of hunting and shooting, Milnes filled it with books – including his large collection of pornography – and with colourfully assorted assemblages of friends for long, talkative visits, filled with readings and play actings and indoor games, fuelled by heavy eating and drinking.

But for the time being Milnes's effective home was to be London, where he moved into his rooms at 26 Pall Mall in 1827, the year in which he was returned to Parliament for Pontefract. At that point he was a conservative, an adherent of Peel. He was not regarded as a serious political figure by Peel or anyone else in politics. His speeches were pompous and grandiloquent. But he was generally liked. Disraeli, another politician with one foot in the world of literature, was, as I have said, an exception. He made a very disobliging remark about Milnes as a host, in the guise of Mr Vavasour in *Tancred*: 'Whatever your creed, class or country, one might almost add your character, you were a welcome guest at his matutinal meal, provided you were celebrated. That qualification, however, was rigidly enforced.' That was unfair, dogs of various degrees of lameness were frequently to be seen. But a major point of Milnes's breakfasts was the presence of *some* lions for everyone else to admire.

Milnes did have one unrelenting and determined enemy in a creature of Disraeli's, George Smythe, later Lord Strangford. In 1849 Milnes was provoked into challenging Smythe to a duel. Perhaps luckily for Milnes the event never came off, although it remains obscure how the matter was settled. Even those who were not attracted by Milnes's gaiety, amusingness and good nature and solemn souls who disapproved of his levity seem seldom to have thought him worse than comical.

The surface of Milnes's political career is certainly unimpressive. He stuck to Peel until Peel fell in 1846 and then transferred his loyalty to Palmerston and the Whigs. But there is more consistency in his politics than that suggests. He was always in favour of reform, improvement and the alleviation of suffering. He supported the repeal of the Corn Laws in this Tory period, he was critical of the royal family and turned into something like a republican, he wanted more democracy, supported the North in the American Civil War when most powerful people in England were enthusiasts for the South, wanted the destruction of Napoleon III but deplored the way in which Bismarck brought him down.

Once he was installed in London, Milnes gathered a large circle of friendly ladies around him. Among them were 'unfortunates' like Lady Blessington at Gore House with the Count d'Orsay in attendance and Caroline Norton, one of the three beautiful Sheridan sisters, who had been edged out of respectable society by the suit brought by her husband against Melbourne. Not of the demi-monde but not of the beau monde either was the wife of George Grote, utilitarian and historian of Greece, a most entertaining and intelligent woman, who was devoted to Milnes.

Milnes married, although only at the age of forty-two, his wife being a comfortably mature thirty-seven, and they had three children. There is no evidence of previous attachments, unless the emotionally vigorous friendships with his Cambridge contemporaries can be so described. Travelling in Turkey he had been to see dancing girls, and that may not have been a purely spectatorial form of entertainment. Then there is the matter of his large accumulation of erotica. That does not seem to have started in earnest until the late 1850s, when Milnes had been married for a number of years and was getting near fifty years of age. It is, after all, an old man's vice.

The crucial event for him – and in a way for us – of the first years of finding his feet in London was his meeting with Carlyle, which took place soon after Milnes's installation in that city. Carlyle was a combative person with a temper rendered uncertain by dyspepsia. He preached and practised a doctrine of work. Yet he was and remained deeply fond of the apparently unemployed and frivolous Milnes. There are two explanations for this – one kinder than the other – and there is probably truth in both of them.

First, on a crudely practical basis, Milnes was useful to Carlyle in introducing him to grand and fashionable people. Carlyle, to the acute displeasure of his wife, enjoyed the company of aristocratic women, in particular that of Lady Harriet Baring, later Lady Ashburton. In 1838 Milnes's old Trinity friend, Spedding, helped Carlyle to recruit Milnes into their campaign to create the London Library. He had, as they did not, the knowledge and influence to get some noble and famous names involved so that they would attract others of their kind on to the subscription list. As we now realise, it was quite a close shave and Carlyle at times seemed to despair of it. But it was not for lack of effort on Milnes's part that the scheme seemed to hang for a time in the balance.

In 1840 he started a long connection with the Hotel Meurice in Paris, his home there on many subsequent visits. Montalembert, made friends with in Rome, took him to visit the salons of Lamartine, preparing himself for brief greatness in 1848, and Thiers. He met George Sand and began a long, communicative friendship with de Tocqueville. In England he heard Liszt play at Lady Blessington's and stayed with Sydney Smith at Combe Florey.

Milnes, for all his liberal, democratic, broadly republican sympathies, loved grand parades and ceremonies. He attended the fairly catastrophic Eglinton Tournament in Scotland. It was the first of a series of such outings. Republican or not, in 1842 he went dressed up as Chaucer, a good choice in respect of shape and size, to the State Fancy Dress Ball devised by Prince Albert in aid of the distressed Spitalfields weavers. Later on he took a conspicuous part in the Paris Exhibition of 1867 and was present at the opening of the Suez Canal in 1869.

In 1842 on a visit to Egypt he met Mehemet Ali, who was running the country independently of its nominal Turkish overlord. In *Palm Leaves*, a poetic record of his travels at this time, he condemned westernization as an unmixed evil. Greece, revisited after eleven years, disappointed him in the way de Valera's republic of shopkeepers disappointed the partisans of Irish freedom. The boat he took up the Nile was called *Zuleika*, a quite appropriate bit of prospective fancy. On the way back home he called in, characteristically, on King Louis Philippe. Still a Tory by normal allegiance, he supported the social reform legislation of Ashley (later Shaftesbury).

His father, as a result of a nasty riding accident in 1840, became less mobile and more eccentric for the considerable remainder of his life. He was not too confused, however, to fail to secure £100,000 from railway companies needing bits of his land. His son, getting nowhere in politics, managed to bear the success of his friend Gladstone, who gravely discouraged him from trying to get a post in the British embassy in Paris as being negatively motivated by the desire to get out of British politics. Disraeli's parallel success, both in politics and literature, was harder to endure.

Travel as usual assuaged his disappointments. In Berlin he

met the aged Alexander von Humboldt but was kept away from the king as a suspicious character, made friends with Varnhagen von Ense, who encouraged his hobby of autograph collecting, and Bettina von Arnim. He was able to indulge in Goethe worship. On his return he wrote a sound article on the political state of Prussia for the *Edinburgh Review*, correctly predicting revolution. Late in the decade he was in Spain and Portugal.

Another way of forgetting himself was to look after the welfare of others. As Henry Adams, a severe critic of the human race, observed in praise of Milnes, 'He made it his business to be kind'. He procured a civil list pension for Tennyson, who was in financial difficulties, but was, all the same, not pleased. He got a job for the desperate Coventry Patmore in the British Museum. He came to the assistance of Thomas Hood and, when he died, of his family. Although he said he preferred individual to collective philanthropy, he supported the bill for the improvement of the college at Maynooth for the training of Roman Catholic priests in Ireland and wrote a pamphlet calling for the subsidisation of the Catholic church in Ireland. Visiting Ireland to see the famine at first hand, he was sharply observant of the continuing luxury in the great houses of the ascendancy.

His turn to Palmerston and the Whigs, when Peel fell in 1846, meant he had to resign from the Carlton Club. However, the gates of Woburn were now open to him as a compensation. His constant visits to the mansions of the nobility did not prevent him from describing the aristocrats of England as stupid and helpless. And his increasing fondness for democracy did not extend to embracing any kind of socialism. In favouring a wider franchise, he was going against his own interests, for he hated the often narrowly run elections he had to undergo in the comparatively rotten borough of Pontefract. His support of Corn Law repeal was also a work of self-denial for one who depended for the lavish comforts he found indispensable on rents from agricultural land.

The events of 1848, which he had correctly predicted in his article on Prussia a few years before, drew him to France to see his friend Lamartine in full, if brief, oratorical frenzy. His attitude as a jovial spectator of the revolution caused some annoyance. It is no surprise to find him, once back in England, calling on the exiled Metternich. He wrote a pamphlet criticising the failure of the British government to assist the revolutionary movements in continental Europe. It was George Smythe's cruel review of this that led to their unconsummated duel. Milnes was oppressed by the violent reaction to the uprisings of 1848 and gave aid to the refugees who fled to England from it.

Of more lasting significance, however, was the publication of his *Life of Keats*, to which I shall return later. He was now forty but seemed older. People remarked how he seemed to have no upper teeth. He was certainly getting rather fat and embarked around this time on a long series of visits to spas to counteract this tendency and the gout by which he was increasingly afflicted. His physical state impaired neither a newly arisen idea of getting married nor considerable success with an improbable fiancée, Florence Nightingale. There is no doubt at all that she returned his affection; probably she felt it more strongly than he did. She spoke with feeling, if in a rather cumbrous way, of 'his genius of friendship in philanthropy.' It was surely better for both of them that the proposal was in the end declined.

Instead, in 1851 he married Annabelle Crewe who had been largely brought up in the country by an aunt. It was hardly ideal training for the hectic social life at Fryston and in London and the frequent travel that lay ahead of her. In fact she seems to have coped pretty well, although she became sickly, bowed and rather melancholic in later life. Milnes's long immersion in an intensely bachelor existence in no way made him an inconsiderate husband. His established mode of life continued. As a married man he moved from his rooms in Pall Mall to a house in Upper Brook Street. But his friends commented on his constant solicitousness for Annabelle's well-being. His old tutor, Thirlwall, now a bishop, slightly regretted the move from Pall Mall. 'It is very likely – nay certain – that you will still collect agreeable people about your wife's breakfast table; but can I ever sit down there without the certainty that I shall meet with none but respectable persons?' By and large the marriage, held together by solid and continuing affection rather than passion, seems to have been happy. Annabelle adjusted herself to the constant social activity of Upper Brook Street and Fryston (ominously labelled 'Freezetown' by Tennyson), but she did rather draw the line at Swinburne. She accompanied Milnes on many of his travels. She gave birth to daughters in 1852 and 1855 and a son, Robert, in 1858, the later Marquess of Crewe. She died in 1874, eleven years before her husband.

In the years of their marriage, Napoleon III became emperor. 'My old breakfaster,' as Milnes called him, had often visited him in the 1840s. Disraeli recalled private conversations with him in a conveniently private bow-window in the Pall Mall rooms in that period. On one occasion he, Disraeli, Kinglake, Suleiman Pasha, Richard Cobden and Count d'Orsay were in the wildly assorted group of guests. Cobden described d'Orsay as 'a fleshy, animal-like creature'. Napoleon's seizure of power aroused fears of an invasion in England. Milnes rose to the occasion, discharging his commission with the 2nd West Riding Regiment of Militia in drilling the locals who had been called to the colours. There was a sartorial benefit from this public duty, an ornate red uniform, even unembellished as it was by anything in the way of decorations, which was to serve him well in various ceremonial events later on.

During the 1850s the arrival of several notable Americans in England gave Milnes the opportunity to display his interest in and good feelings towards the United States. This attitude was directly opposed to the generally mocking and contemptuous view of America and the Americans that then prevailed in England. It had been memorably expressed in the 1840s in Dickens's *American Notes* and *Martin Chuzzlewit*. As long before as 1838 Milnes had written in the *London and Westminster Review* a long article about Emerson, in which he explained the distinguishing peculiarities of American English, which then, as now, excited ridicule in England, as being due to persistence of uneliminated residues of Elizabethan idiom.

Ten years later Emerson, travelling in England, met Milnes for the first time and wrote warmly about him: 'Milnes is everywhere and knows everything. . . . His good humour is infinite . . . He is very liberal of his money and sincerely kind and useful to young people of merit.' Hawthorne, extremely sensitive to English slights, found Milnes 'pleasant and sensible', but, he went on, 'an intellectual and refined American is a higher man than he – a higher and a finer one.' In an agreeable comment on Milnes's physical appearance, Hawthorne said Milnes resembled Longfellow 'though of a thicker build'. That calls to mind the fine observation of William James's son who, called on to describe what an acquaintance looked like, replied 'like Jesus Christ, but thicker set'. Milnes certainly laid on a good selection of lions at one breakfast to which Hawthorne came: Lord Lansdowne, Robert and Elizabeth Barrett Browning, Macaulay, Florence Nightingale's mother and, perhaps for reassurance, his countryman, George Ticknor.

Milnes was one of the first people in England to recognise the merits of Walt Whitman and eventually called on him when, in 1875 after his wife's death, he visited the U.S. During that trip Milnes also called on General Sherman in St Louis and renewed his acquaintance with Emerson, who by then, although 'easy to talk to' was no longer able to write. Milnes, as I have mentioned earlier, was something of a rarity for his support of the Northern side in the Civil War. Recollection of the fact may have augmented the general enthusiasm with which he was received over there years afterwards.

During the early years of the Civil War the young Henry Adams, then twenty-three, was serving with the American embassy in London as secretary to his father, the minister. Depressed by the Whig government's recognition of the sovereign status of the Confederacy, he went to stay at fog-bound Fryston where Milnes had as guests only his friend Stirling, Laurence Oliphant and an extraordinary looking child who turned out in fact to be Swinburne and who put on an enthralling performance after dinner. Henry Adams never forgot Milnes's protective kindness and wrote of it in his autobiography many years later.

The friendship of the two men had another interesting literary consequence. When Henry James arrived in London in 1827 he had a letter of introduction for Milnes from Henry Adams in his pocket. Milnes got ahead of him by inviting him to a breakfast party before he had managed to present it. Milnes took him to a club where he met Trollope and then had him to stay at Fryston, where Tennyson, Gladstone and Schliemann were also staying. James did something to return this abundant hospitality by giving Milnes, in his turn, a letter of introduction to Flaubert and Turgenev. Goodwill manages to prevail over superciliousness in James's description of Milnes:

> a battered and world-wrinkled old mortal, with a restless and fidgety vanity, but with an immense fund of real kindness and humane feeling. He is not personally fascinating, though as a general thing he talks very well, but I like his sociable, democratic, sympathetic, inquisitive old temperament. Half the human race, certainly everyone that one has ever heard of, appears sooner or later to have stayed at Fryston Hall.

Milnes soon followed up the introduction to Flaubert and Turgenev and on the same visit to Paris added Zola and Daudet to his list of acquaintances.

40

In 1853 he was one of the three founders of the Philobiblion Society, a serious and energetic group of book-lovers, thirty five in number: noblemen with great inherited libraries, scholars, writers, even publishers. In the season in London it met once or twice a month and Milnes was active in the production of its *Miscellanies*, of which fifteen were published in the thirty-one years of the society's existence. It died in 1884, a year before Milnes did.

He was an incessant book collector but the part of his collection that has most caught public attention is its pornographic element. For the rest it was by no means confined to expensive rarities. Leigh Hunt praised it for its democratic hospitableness, describing it as 'the concentration of infinite bookstalls'. Nor was his library for show. Milnes was constantly reading and was always up-to-date on the most recently published books. When Fryston was burnt down in 1875 Milnes was away in Ireland. Most of the books were got out but many of them, as is commonly the case, had been drenched by the firemen's hoses. Returning to find many sets incomplete and many books damaged, he said, 'my Dante and Froissart have turned up but Charles I's Spenser is still missing.'

Reflecting Milne's love of the famous, there were many items of association interest – among them a piece of Voltaire's dressing gown, a presentation cup from Goethe, Richard Burton's passport to Mecca and the visitors' book from Burns's cottage at Alloway. A large place in the collection was taken up by books on the French Revolution, books of nineteenth-century poetry, works on theology, books on music, witchcraft and crime. With its group of works on school punishment we approach the pornographic area.

His pornographic library was, in what we must, I suppose, regard as a characteristically English style, very strong on flagellation. Milnes's taste for this was presumably not founded on experience. Unlike Swinburne he had not revelled in being on the receiving end of beatings at school. There was a lot of French eighteenth-century material. To acquire it he relied on the services of an intriguingly shadowy figure: Fred Hanley. The only son of a general who had served with distinction in Malta, he had settled in Paris towards the end of the 1840s, with a mistress whose constant presence inhibited his social movements in England. The Goncourt brothers had met him and been delightedly shocked by the depth of his sadistic obsession.

Milnes's relations with him were more businesslike. A constant flow of beautifully produced erotic rubbish was conveyed to him in England, by means of elaborate strategems designed to evade the attentions of the customs officers. Some came across with a Queen's Messenger en route to Palmerston, others in the diplomatic bag from the embassy in Paris to the Foreign Office; others again by the helpful hand of the manager of Covent Garden. Milnes brought another new friend with an interest in the obscene, Richard Burton, into touch with Hanley, and the intrepid traveller undertook to get him a flayed human skin from Dahomey.

Milnes's more virtuous impulses continued to operate. After the death by drowning of his friend Warburton, he came to the assistance of his widow and two young sons. Carlyle, who had been somewhat estranged by Milnes's championing of Keats, soon warmed to him again and recruited him in the attempt to do something for the widow of Leigh Hunt. He came to the support of J. A. Froude, first at the time of the storm and expulsion from his Oxford fellowship which followed the publication of his *Nemesis of Faiths*, again when he applied, unsuccessfully in 1857, for a history professorship in Oxford and once again when his biography of Carlyle excited wide displeasure. He played some part in getting the increase in stipend for the Rev. Arthur Nicholls which made it possible for him to marry Charlotte Brontë. He was busy on behalf of more generalised humanitarian purposes – such as stopping the cruel punishments to which sailors were subjected at sea (a fact that suggests that his interest in flagellation did not extend to approving of it in practice), the relief of fallen women and the repeal of the Contagious Diseases Act.

In 1856 Palmerston offered Milnes's father a peerage which Robert Milnes refused, to the intense regret of his son. Two years later he died, still true in his old Tory loyalty, now attached to Disraeli and Derby, and cheerfully disagreeing with his son. He had received a wider education than Milnes and was given to pointing out grammatical slips and misuses of words in the writings that Milnes sent him. At last in 1863 Milnes was made a peer on his own account, taking the title of Lord Houghton. Palmerston had offered him a minor Treasury post some time before, and in the most courteous way, but Milnes realised he would look foolish, in the light of his known political ambitions, to accept it. Even so Disraeli said of him that he was too ridiculous to be made a peer.

He kept up his progressive interests in the House of Lords. As well as the humanitarian issues I mentioned earlier which belong to this period of his career, he supported the resolution for enlarging the franchise in the middle 1860s which culminated in the Reform Act of 1867.

Travel and sociability continued to the end of his life, which appropriately took place in a spa. After the age of fifty his gout became progressively worse, and he was accidently dragged off his horse in Hyde Park in 1877 and was laid up for a week. In 1872 he reviewed *Middlemarch* at length in the *Edinburgh Review*. He led the movement after Dickens's death in 1870 to have him buried in Westminster Abbey. His poetic muse made a final, desperate emergence from retirement in 1873 on the occasion of Livingstone's death:

The swarthy followers stood aloof,
    Unled – unfathered;
He lay beneath that grassy roof,
    Fresh-gathered.
He bade them, as they pass the hut
    To give no warning
Of their still faithful presence, but
    'Good Morning'.

Morning of sympathy and trust
    For such as bore
Their master's spirit's sacred crust
    To England's shore.

Eating and drinking excessively to the last, he managed to live to the age of seventy-six without any catastrophic loss of powers. After the opening of the Suez Canal in 1869 he was in Paris in 1872 to see what the Germans and the Communards had done to it. He was in Italy in 1874 and, as has been mentioned, in the United States (by way of Canada) in 1875, and in Ireland when his home burned down two years later. Early in the 1880s he made a final trip to Germany and, naturally, met von Moltke and the Austrian crown prince who was to die at Mayerling. He was in Cairo and Athens (where he had a heart attack) in 1882 and in Rome in 1883 and 1885, the year of his death. Busy to the end, he had just unveiled busts to Coleridge in Westminster Abbey and to Thomas Gray at Pembroke College, Cambridge.

It had been a full and active life, a somewhat superficial one, perhaps, but carried on all over the world, in all sorts of company, often for humane and decent public purposes and unremittingly for the pursuit of the pleasure of individuals and, through it, of his own. Milnes did no harm, a lot of good and was the cause of a great deal of fun. Three lasting achievements stand to his credit.

The first, and most important, is his reclamation of Keats from oblivion and disapproval. For people born in the twentieth century, although they are aware of Keats's misfortunes with critics in his lifetime, the idea that there could ever have been a time, after his death, when he was not recognised to be one of England's major poets must come as a surprise. His poems had been republished in two volumes in 1841, twenty years after his death, but had attracted no notice except from the young Rossetti and Holman Hunt. Where there was not simple ignorance there was intense reprobation: the sensual richness of Keats's verse was seen as the expression of a weak, unhealthy and, worst of all, pagan character.

Milnes did not deny the paganism. For the most part he let Keats speak for himself through his poems and letters, supplemented by the recollections Milnes had assembled of the people who had known him. The conception of Keats as a brilliantly gifted poet and a courageous and dignified man came steadily to be established as a result of Milnes's work, so that it is hard to imagine the derelict state of his reputation at the time Milnes set himself to putting matters right.

Sensuality and paganism were also features of the other important poet well served by Milnes. In this case the service needed to be direct and personal since Swinburne, without some managerial or avuncular figure in charge of him, was bound to go off the rails. Milnes set him going in the right direction poetically. It has been suggested that he encouraged Swinburne to try his hand at Greek tragedy rather than boisterous imitation – thus giving rise to *Atalanta in Calydon*. He brought Swinburne into the world, away from his feverish and drunken isolation, among other things arranging a meeting with an early hero of Swinburne's, Landor, which turned out to be almost ecstatically rewarding. He helped him get his poetry and reviews published. In the six years in which they were close, before Swinburne turned away from his mentor, fired by an infatuation with the revolutionary ideals of Mazzini, the best of Swinburne's early poetry was composed.

Swinburne was intemperate with his pen as well as the bottle. In his huge novel *Lesbia Brandon* there is a morally unwholesome charcter, Mr Linley, who has much in common, at least in some of his opinions, tastes and manners of speech, with Milnes. Could John Buchan, in his Yellow Book period, have got a look at the manuscript of the book or its unpublished proofs? That would allow for the resurrection of Mr Linley as Mr Andrew Lumley of the *Power House*, the evil, magnetic, soft-spoken tycoon and collector from whom the thin fabric of civilisation is at risk.

Milnes's final service is, of course, something which this lecture is designed to commemorate: his work for the London Library. Not only did he assist Carlyle at the outset by drawing in some high-ranking personages so as to attract the attention of others of their kind. He continued to be involved in its affairs for the rest of his life. In 1857, for example, he was under pressure from a Miss Agnes Stickland to secure the appointment as librarian of the very minor poet, Alaric Watts.

I like to think that there is really more of his spirit about the place than there is of grim old Carlyle's. We all know that the gospel of work is honoured in it, not least from the enormous array of tributes to the place in the acknowledgements pages of books that have been written in it or based on its resources. It is very much a library for enjoyment as well as use, like Milnes's own, though I should not want to press that comparison too far. If Richard Monckton Milnes cannot quite claim to be the emblem of the library he can at least be the genial reverse of the medal whose obverse is the stern, commanding visage of his loving friend Carlyle.

GEORGE ELIOT

1819–1880

AND

GEORGE HENRY LEWES

1817–1878

_____

A.S. BYATT

GEORGE ELIOT AND
GEORGE HENRY LEWES

I OFTEN ASK MYSELF – both as a reader and with a kind of novelist's curiosity – what would have happened to the English, and indeed the European novel, if George Eliot had married Herbert Spencer, as in 1852 she desperately wanted to do. Some of her letters to him were first printed in 1976.

> I want to know if you can assure me that you will not forsake me, that you will always be with me as much as you can and share your thoughts and feelings with me. If you become attached to someone else, then I must die, but until then I could gather courage to work and make life valuable, if only I had you near me. I do not ask you to sacrifice anything – I would be very good and cheerful and never annoy you . . . I have struggled – indeed I have – to renounce everything and be entirely unselfish, but I find myself utterly unequal to it. Those who have known me best have always said, that if ever I loved anyone thoroughly my whole life must turn upon that feeling, and I find they said truly.

This is, as Gordon Haight points out, not the letter of a romantic young girl but of a desperately serious and dignified woman of thirty-two. Spencer liked but could not love her, and told a friend much later (1881): 'Her feelings became involved and mine did not. The lack of physical attraction was fatal.

Strongly as my judgment prompted my instincts would not respond.'[1]

He even came, he claims, to feel that he should possibly offer marriage, 'even without positive affection on my part, but this she at once saw would lead to unhappiness'. But she insisted that they went on seeing each other – and then one day Spencer took with him G. H. Lewes, whom she already knew 'slightly' and after a time Lewes took to remaining behind when Spencer left, and after a further time, Lewes and Marian Evans took the decision to live publicly together as man and wife. They could not marry, as Lewes was already married, and had condoned his wife's adultery with his friend Thornton Hunt by continuing to support her children by him. The rest of the story of that most successful of non-marriages has often been told. They moved from ostracism to Royal Visits and almost being mobbed at the Westminster Abbey wedding of Tennyson's son.

Mrs Gaskell, on discovering that the author of *Adam Bede* was a woman, and living in sin, asked the publisher George Smith, '*How came she to like Mr Lewes so much?* I know he has his good points but somehow he is so soiled for a woman like her to fancy.' She wrote Eliot a generous letter of praise ending forthrightly: 'I should not be quite true in my ending, if I did not say before I concluded that I wish you *were* Mrs Lewes. However that cannot be helped, as far as I can see, and one must not judge others.'[2]

If Herbert Spencer was monumentally serious and self-satisfied, Lewes was quick, various, racy, risqué, curiously inno-cent as well as 'so soiled', a professional journalist, typically Victorian in that that made him interested in everything. It is

---

[1] *The George Eliot Letters* (1840–70) Vol. 8, ed Gordon Haight.
[2] *The Letters of Mrs Gaskell* (1966), ed J. A. Chapple and A. Pollard.

by now a matter of general knowledge that we owe the novels of George Eliot at least in part to George Lewes's encouragement and protection of her talent. He did not discover it – she was both a powerful woman of letters and had tried her hand at fiction before they began to live together. But whereas she had to tell Spencer that she was not ashamed of her desperate letter because 'I am conscious that in the light of reason and true refinement I am worthy of your respect and tenderness, whatever gross men or vulgarminded women might think of me,' with Lewes she had both love, affection, intellectual companionship, protection from social fears, lightheartedness, intelligent admiration of what she was and could do, and shrewd business advice. He extended her horizons, let her relax and be herself. She was so morbidly afraid of criticism, at least as a novelist, that if he had not protected her from it, and given her justified praise, I am quite sure we would have had both fewer and less ambitious books from her.

I don't want to talk about Lewes's management of his wife's career. I want to talk today about Lewes's own ideas and writings, and what they brought to the novels of George Eliot. I have become suspicious of the studies of literary influence on which I was fed as a student. I know very well that any little echo of an idea from Lewes's work to that of George Eliot could be matched by all sorts of equally interesting echoes from other sources and voices, in both of them, that will go unmentioned. This isn't a scholarly lecture – it's a kind of readerly reconstruction of the serious and amiable and very long dialogue that went on between those two, day in, day out, for almost thirty years, until she wrote, at his death, in her Diary, 'Here I and sorrow sit'. I want to talk about Lewes's *variety* and how that variety helps us to understand the huge changes his wife made in the form of the novel itself.

Lewes wrote indefatigably about everything. He was both actor and playwright, and a regular theatre critic. He wrote two novels, one of which, *Rose, Blanche and Violet*, Marian Evans could not be bothered to finish at the time of her passion for Spencer. He was one of the best reviewers of the novel of his time, ready to stick his neck out and write intelligent praise of the unknown Currer Bell, ready to single out an American sea-story, *The Whale*, largely ignored or dismissed by other reviewers, as part, with Poe and Hawthorne, of a real new American literature. He was a good editor (of the *Fortnightly*). He wrote what is still arguably the best biography of Goethe. He understood Balzac. He wrote a very readable *Biographical History of Philosophy*, covering the Greeks, the Enlightenment and the German, French and English nineteenth centuries, but ignoring the middle ages on the grounds that their philosophy was mere theology and religion. He also wrote popular books on the physiology of common life, and the delightful *Sea-side Studies* on marine biology, and the pleasures of hunting for polyps and anemones. He popularised both Auguste Comte and Charles Darwin with enthusiasm (though his enthusiasm for Comte waned). He saw himself as a serious scientist, and believed he had made genuine discoveries about the nervous system. His *magnum opus, Problems of Life and Mind,* I have taken out of the London Library repeatedly and have never been able to read. He became a member of the committee of the Library in 1867. In *Sea-side Studies,* he described his 1857 voyage to the Scilly Isles with George Eliot, who finished *Mr Gilfil* there. He wrote: 'A century ago on the 25th May 1752, Borlase, the admirable antiquarian, whose *Observations on the Ancient and Present State of the Scilly Islands* was among my books, set sail in the sloop Godolphin at 7 in the morning and about 9 in the evening drew near the islands.' He adds a footnote, 'Thanks to that most convenient and to all students most valuable of institutions, *The London Library*, which manifold experience causes me to urge every man of letters to join.'[1]

John Wells in his history of the Library says Lewes must have been its ideal member with his eclectic interests and enthusiasms, and certainly if we read George Eliot's accounts of their evening readings to each other we can see that however many books they owned, the Library must have been a necessity. George Eliot recalls their readings in her journal, written on Jersey during the same voyage:

> Our readings aloud were Cromwell's Letters, *Aurora Leigh* (for the 2d time), *Life of Charlotte Brontë*, Maury's *Physical Geography of the Sea*, *Twelfth Night* and *Macbeth*, and *Northanger Abbey* and *Persuasion*. I read the *Oedipus Tyrannus* and the *Oedipus Colonnus*, de Quincey's *Glories of Stage Coach Travelling* and *Revolt of the Tartars* and the greater part of Shelley's poems.[2]

Earlier in East Sheen, in 1855 she wrote:

> I think we like East Sheen better and better, and are happier every day, writing hard, walking hard, reading Homer and science and rearing tadpoles. I read aloud for about three hours every evening, beginning with Boswell's Johnson, or some such enjoyable book, not unfriendly to digestion, then subsiding into the dreary dryness of Whewell's *History of the Inductive Sciences* and winding up with Heine's wit and imagination. We breakfast at ½ past 8, read to ourselves till 10, write till ½ past 1, walk till nearly 4, and dine at 5, regretting each day as it goes.[3]

When the two of them first set out publicly together for Germany in 1854, Lewes was working on his *Life of Goethe*. This is arguably

[1] G. H. Lewes *Sea-side Studies* (1858)
[2] George Eliot *Letters* Vol. 2
[3] George Eliot *Letters* Vol. 2

his greatest achievement, and Eliot's presence and help are an essential part of it. She translated some of Goethe's verse for him, and he offered her concealed tributes in his text. Writing of Goethe's abandonment of Frederika he says:

> Had he loved her enough to share a life with her, his experience of woman might have been less extensive, but it would assuredly have gained an element it wanted. It would have been deepened. He had experienced, and he could paint (no one better) the exquisite devotion of woman to man; but he had scarcely ever felt the peculiar tenderness of man for woman, when that tenderness takes the form of vigorous protecting fondness. He knew little, and that not until late in life, of the subtle interweaving of habit with affection, which makes life saturated with love, and love itself become dignified through the serious aims of life. He knew little of the exquisite *companionship* of two souls striving in emulous spirit of loving rivalry to become better, to become wiser, teaching each other to soar.[1]

Lewes and Eliot were European writers, happy in French, German, Italian, Spanish, Greek and Latin, and reading the *Goethe* is a useful corrective to the British tendency to see Eliot simply as a successor of Jane Austen. Lewes's description of Faust and Mephistopheles riding across a barren heath and hearing the carpenters building the scaffold for Margaret's execution for infanticide reminds us that Hetty's agony in *Adam Bede* has its universal moral roots in European Romantic vision, as well as in Eliot's aunt's terrible local experience. The seeds of *Daniel Deronda* were also sown on this journey, I think. A connection that has always particularly interested me is that between the *tableaux vivants* enacted by Gwendolen and those put on by the frivolously sentimental, emotionally corrupt aristocrat, Luciane,

[1] G. H. Lewes *Life of Goethe* (Everyman 1908)

in Goethe's *Elective Affinities*. George Eliot in Berlin in 1854 records her pleasure in seeing a painting by Jan Steen, 'which Goethe describes in the *Wahlverwandtschaften* as the model of a *tableau vivant*, presented by Luciane and her friends. It is the daughter being reproved by her father while the mother is emptying her wine-glass.'[1] On this journey, too, Eliot through Lewes met both Varnhagen von Ense, who was a friend of Goethe and had been married to the great Jewish actress, Rahel, and Liszt, who enchanted her by his playing and his conversation. Out of all this, and out of Lewes's knowledge of the theatre, come all the theatrical themes of *Daniel Deronda*, the Alchirisi, with a man's genius burning in a woman's body, Daniel's mother, the musician Klesmer with his sense of true work and true worth and local eccentricities, and the vapid parodies of true painting and drama enacted in the bored country gentry's amateur, imitative, static 'performances'.

When the *Goethe* was being written, George Eliot's fiction was still to be written, but I think the influence of Lewes's carefully thought out, and very *practical* views of the art of narrative, can be seen to be at work in her early tales particularly. He writes approvingly of *Werther* as he writes approvingly of Jane Austen, of whom he said:

It is only plenitude of power that restrains her from the perils of the form she has chosen – the perils, namely, of tedium and commonplace . . . She makes her people speak and act as they speak and act in everyday life; and she is the only artist who has done this with success.[2]

He praises the same virtues in *Werther*:

Rosenkrantz in the true spirit of that criticism which seeks everywhere for meanings more recondite than the author

[1] J. W. Cross *George Eliot's Life* Vol I (1895)
[2] Quoted in Richard Stang *The Theory of the Novel in England 1850–70* (1959)

dreamt of – thinks that Goethe exhibits great art in making Werther a diplomatist, because a diplomatist is a man of *shams* (Scheintuer); but the truth is, Goethe made him precisely what he found him. His art is truth. He is so great an artist that the simplest realities have to him significance. Charlotte cutting bread and butter for the children – the scene of the ball – the children clinging round Werther for sugar, and pictures of that kind, betray so little inventive power that they have excited the ridicule of some English critics to whom poetry is a thing of pomp, not the beautiful vesture of reality.[1]

George Eliot, defending the local specificity of her depiction of the children in *Amos Barton* against her publisher's desire for something more general and noble and uplifting, is arguing in the same tradition. Indeed, her sure hand with the children in *Adam Bede*, her certainty that the detail is interesting, is part of the same aesthetic strain of thought.

Lewes analysing the *Wahlverwandtschaften* praises Goethe for dramatic presentation, 'without any description or explanation from the author. The whole representation is so objective, so simple, and the march of the story is so quiet, moving among such familiar details, that except in the masterpieces of Miss Austen, I know not where to look for a comparison.' He goes on to comment on the way in which English and French readers may feel wearied by 'the many small details which encumber the march of the story, and irritate the curiosity which is impatient for the denouement.' A friend, he says in the first edition, later changed to –

A great writer, and one very dear to me, thinks that the long episodes which interrupt the progress of the story during the interval of Eduard's absence and return, are artistic devices

[1] G. H. Lewes *Life of Goethe*

for impressing the reader with a sense of the slow movement of life; and, in truth, it is only in fiction that the denouement usually lies close to the exposition. I give this opinion, for the reader's consideration; but it seems to me more ingenious than just.[1]

We can almost overhear these two very intelligent people discussing the form of the novel and its relation to reality – and we can hear the voice of the greatest English depictor of the slow, encumbered movement of life.

Another aspect of Lewes's interest in Goethe which also has interest for students of George Eliot's novels, is his sympathetic, balanced and enthusiastic account of Goethe's compulsive interest in science and in scientific research. Goethe studied physiology, and had a claim to be considered the discoverer of the intermaxillary bone, present in animals, but formerly thought to be absent in man. He studied optics and developed his own anti-Newtonian theory of colour. He wrote a treatise on *The Metamorphoses of Plants* which studied the morphology of plant forms as a development of two primitive elements, 'stem' and 'leaf', into more complex structures. Lewes connected this to more recent studies in Development, which he said was 'quite a modern study. Formerly men were content with the full-statured animal – the perfected art – the completed society. The phases of development and the laws of growth were disregarded, or touched on in a vague uncertain manner . . . [Now, however] In Geology, in Physiology, in History, and in Art, we are all bent on tracing the phases of development. To understand the *grown* we try to follow the *growth*'.[2] *The Origin of Species* was published in 1859, and *In Memoriam*, haunted by ideas of geological and biological change, in 1850. Lewes's own desired image of himself and his own activity comes through his description of

[1] G. H. Lewes *Life of Goethe*
[2] G. H. Lewes *Life of Goethe*

the linked subjects of study. A civilised man should know about geology, physiology, history, sociology and art. At the end of *Sea-side Studies* he observes that the discovery of organisms which reproduced themselves alternately by 'budding' and egg-laying was made by Chamisso.

> In 1819 a Germanised Frenchman, known to all lovers of romance as the author of *Peter Schlemil*, made a discovery in Natural History which was almost as incredible as his Shadowless Man. Whether this will endear the name of Chamisso still more to his admirers may be a question. Literary men will point with some satisfaction to the fact that a novelist was the discoverer of a form of reproduction unsuspected by the profoundest zoologists. They may also remember that the luminous doctrine of plant-morphology was the discovery of the greatest of our modern poets; and that the great Haller himself was a poet and litterateur before, in later life, he devoted himself with such splendid success to physiology.[1]

George Eliot reviewed the *Life of Goethe*, in 1855, with a precisely related scientific metaphor. What is wanted, she says, is an account, descriptive and analytical of the writings, and 'such a *natural history* of his various productions as will show how they were outgrowths of his mind at different stages of its culture'.[2]

She saw her own work as 'natural history' too. One of the great reviews she wrote in the year preceding her first fiction was of Wilhelm Heinrich von Riehl's monumental sociological book, *The Natural History of German Life*.[3] In *The Mill on the Floss* she describes St Ogg's, the town, as 'a continuation and outgrowth of nature . . . which carries the traces of its long growth and history

---

[1] G. H. Lewes *Sea-side Studies* (1858)

[2] *The Leader* VI (3 November 1855)

[3] Reprinted in *Selected Essays and other Writings of George Eliot*, ed. A. S. Byatt and Nicholas Warren (Penguin 1990)

like a millennial tree'. In her first fiction she turned naturally to images from science, from physiology and nature study. One of her publisher, Blackwood's, friends was convinced that the unknown author was a man of science. Thomas Noble made a list of phrases and comparisons from *Scenes*: 'as necessary a condition of thought as Time and Space', 'the mental retina', 'the plenum of his own brain', 'the quivering life in a waterdrop', 'a nucleus of healthy life in an organ hardening by disease', 'subtle nerve filaments which elude scientific lenses'. In one phrase in *Janet's Repentance* she brings physiological development strikingly together with historical and moral development in a passage typical of her moral comment and vision, to which I want to return later.

> Nevertheless Evangelicalism had brought into palpable existence and operation in Milby society that idea of duty, that recognition of something to be lived for beyond the mere satisfaction of self, which is to the moral life what the addition of a great central ganglion is to animal life. No man can begin to mould himself on a faith or an idea without rising to a higher order of experience: a principle of subordination, of self-mastery, has been introduced into his nature: he is no longer a mere bundle of impressions, desires and impulses.[1]

Writing of Dissent in Milby she observes that 'Methodism was only to be detected, as you detect curious larvae, by diligent search in dirty corners.'

I have written elsewhere of how her reading of Ruskin at Tenby, coupled with their scientific study, gave her a desire to combine what she defined as Ruskin's *'realism'* – 'the doctrine that all truth and beauty are to be attained by a humble and faithful study of nature' – with the 'desire to know the names of

[1] George Eliot *Scenes of Clerical Life* (1858)

59

things' which is 'to escape from all vagueness and inaccuracy into the daylight of distinct, vivid ideas'.[1] By the time she came to write *Middlemarch* the scientific ideas had become an essential part of the plot of the novel in the honourable but failed ambitions of Lydgate, the medical man who wanted to continue the researches of Bichat into the primitive tissues out of which all other tissues are developed. Much has been written and will continue to be written about the brilliant and intricate metaphorical structure of *Middlemarch*. I should like simply to comment on the interrelation of two patterns which cross and interconnect throughout the novel – the web, and the intricate relations of eyes and light. Eliot uses the metaphor of the web to describe the social medium in which all her individuals are caught, the life of Middlemarch itself, the trap spun for Lydgate in the interweaving of his glances with Rosamund's, so that Eliot remarks on his first feeling 'the hampering thread-like pressure of small social conditions, and their frustrating complexity'. But the web, in turn, is also connected to the many physiological images of the tissues of the body, so that the red *cloth* which Dorothea sees in St Peter's is 'spreading itself everywhere like a disease of the retina' (a kind of web over the eye) and the authorial description of Bichat's ideas compares his nervous tissues – earlier described as 'certain primary webs or tissues' – to spun and woven *cloth*.

> This great seer did not go beyond the consideration of the tissues as ultimate facts in the living organism, making the limit of anatomical analysis; but it was open to another mind to say, have not these structures some common basis from which they have all started, as your sarsnet, gauze, net, satin and velvet from the raw cocoon? Here would be

[1] See my prefaces to the Penguin editions of *The Mill on the Floss* and *Selected Essays, Poems and Other Writings*.

another light, as of oxy-hydrogen, showing the very grain of things, and revising all former explanations.[1]

Lewes compares Bichat's discoveries to Goethe's – and it is worth remarking in parenthesis that *Elective Affinities* itself gets its strange title, and its dramatic form, from the behaviour of molecules as they combine and recombine, used as a metaphor to understand the quasi-automatic amatory patterns of choice of Goethe's specimen characters.

It is often remarked that the character of Will Ladislaw in *Middlemarch* owes much to Lewes, in that he is a lightweight man of many parts, mercurial sympathies, a journalist with artistic sympathies who can turn his hand to anything, a *fluid* 'new man' who represents a new age where men are not statically fixed by social inheritance. It is true that George Eliot did not use her own experience in her fiction until it was long past and formed in her mind – the fiction she wrote at the time of her elopement with Lewes was about her father's memories (*Scenes*), her father's world and her aunt's (*Adam Bede*), her own childhood (*The Mill on the Floss*), followed by more distant works based on thought and literary and philosophical sources – *Silas, Romola, The Spanish Gypsy* and *Felix Holt*. A reader of Eliot's biography and *Middlemarch* might indeed compare Will's lively *responsiveness* to Lewes's as a solution for the cold misery into which Dorothea's idealistic marriage – and her lack of consideration of basic sexual facts about human nature – had led her. Henry James was wrong to say Dorothea needed 'a trooper' after Casaubon – what she needed was exactly Ladislaw. But the other 'hero' of that novel, imperfect as all the characters are, Lydgate, would not have been as he is without George Henry Lewes's passionate dissection of nerve tissues under the microscope. It is of Lydgate that Eliot makes the remark which I felt as a liberation, about how little

[1] George Eliot *Middlemarch* (1871–2)

61

attention we pay to passions of the mind as opposed to 'telling over and over again how a man comes to fall in love with a woman and be wedded to her or else fatally parted from her'. We are, she says, 'comparatively uninterested in that other kind of "makdom and fairnesse" which must be wooed with industrious thought and patient renunciation of small desires'. Her description of Lydgate working with his microscope praises the scientific imagination – in this case also the reforming social imagination – in a string of startling and poetic and precise metaphors.

Many men have been praised as vividly imaginative on the strength of their profuseness in indifferent drawing or cheap narration: – reports of very poor talk going on in distant orbs; or portraits of Lucifer coming down on his bad errands as a large ugly man with bat's wings and spurts of phosphorescence; or exaggerations of wantonness that seem to reflect life in a diseased dream. But these kinds of inspiration Lydgate regarded as rather vulgar and vinous compared with the imagination that reveals subtle actions inaccessible by any sort of lens, but tracked in that outer darkness through long pathways of necessary sequence by that inward light which is the last refinement of Energy, capable of bathing even the ethereal atoms in its ideally illuminated space. He for his part had tossed away all cheap inventions where ignorance finds itself able and at ease; he was enamoured of that arduous invention which is the very eye of research, provisionally framing its object and correcting it to more and more exactness of relation; he wanted to pierce the obscurity of those minute processes which prepare human misery and joy, those invisible thoroughfares which are the first lurking-places of anguish, mania, and crime, that delicate poise and transition which determine the growth of happy or unhappy consciousness.[1]

[1] Ibid

Eliot compared her own activity in this novel to that of the scientist with a microscope, and famously told Dr Joseph Payne, in 1876, that her writing was '*simply a set of experiments in life –* an endeavour to see what our thought and emotion may be capable of . . .' [my italics] She went on, however, to qualify this statement in an important way: 'I become more and more timid – with less daring to adopt any formula which does not get itself clothed for me in some human figure and individual experience, and perhaps that is a sign that if I help others to see at all it must be through the medium of art.'[1]

Lewes's *Biographical History of Philosophy* might be seen from a related point of view, in that it is a popularising work in which Lewes seeks to make the ideas he traces across the ages *incarnate*, to use a word Eliot used, in individual stories, of human beings embedded in particular societies at particular points in history, which he saw, like most of his contemporaries, as a form of steady development. Lewes's particular interests throughout the biographical history are the clash between realism and idealism, the problem of whether we can truly know anything about the world outside ourselves and our senses, the problem of the relation of these thoughts to our moral ideas and conduct. I don't have time to go into his spirited accounts of these arguments, though it might be interesting to quote his account of the Greek New Academy and its scepticism.

> The world apart from our consciousness, i.e. the non-ego *qua* non-ego – the world *per se* – is, we may be certain, something utterly different from our world as we know it; for all we know of it is derived through our consciousness of what its effects are on *us*, and our consciousness is obviously only a *state of ourselves*, not a copy of external things.

[1] George Eliot *Letters* Vol. 6

He elaborates this in modern scientific terms:

> If all animals were blind there would be no such thing as *light* because light is a *phenomenon* made up out of the operation of some unknown thing (supposed to be pulsations of air) on the tympanum. If all animals were without their present nerves, or nerves having the same dispositions, there would be no such thing as *pain*, because pain is a *phenomenon* made out of the operation of some external thing on the nerves.
>
> Light, colour, sound, pain, taste, smell, are all states of consciousness and nothing more. Light with all its myriad forms and colours – Sound with its thousandfold life – make Nature what Nature appears to us; but they are only investitures of the mind. Nature is an eternal Darkness – an eternal Silence.[1]

In that eloquence we meet, as I shall suggest later, something akin to George Eliot's eloquence, just as in Lewes's lively description of Spinoza's exile from his religious community we meet not only the Jews of *Daniel Deronda* but the expelled Dissenter, Silas Marner. (George Eliot translated Spinoza's *Ethics* in 1855, but never published them.) In Lewes's account of the Sophists, with whom he was sympathetic, he gives a long quotation from Macaulay's essay on Machiavelli, describing the national and historical relativism of virtue, in which it is amusing to see the germ of the character of that fourteenth-century Florentine and fictive friend of Machiavelli, Eliot's Tito Melema.

Macaulay argues that whilst among the rude nations beyond the Alps the primary virtue was *courage*.

> Amongst the polished Italians, enriched by commerce, governed by law, and passionately attached to literature, everything was done by superiority of intelligence. Their very

[1] G. H. Lewes *Biographical History of Philosophy* (1845–6) Vol. 2

wars, more pacific than the peace of their neighbours, required rather civil than military qualifications. Hence, while courage was the point of honour in other countries, ingenuity became the point of honour in Italy.

From these principles were deduced, by processes strictly analogous, two opposite systems of fashionable morality. Through the greater part of Europe, the vices which peculiarly belong to timid dispositions, and which are the natural defence of weakness, fraud and hypocrisy, have always been most disreputable. On the other hand, the excesses of haughty and daring spirits have been treated with indulgence, and even with respect. The Italians regarded with corresponding lenity those crimes which require self-command, address, quick observation, fertile invention, and profound knowledge of human nature.[1]

Macaulay compares Henry V of England and Francis Sforza and Othello and Iago as types of the two kinds of virtue. It was Lewes, who, much later in Florence in 1860, had the idea while reading about Savonarola that 'his life and times afford fine material for a historical romance. Polly at once caught at the idea with enthusiasm'.[2] One can imagine Tito's Greek cunning springing from Lewes's admiration of Macaulay's insights. Eliot defended the detail of her researched Florentine life to R. H. Hutton by saying, 'It is the habit of my imagination to strive after as full a vision of the medium in which a character moves as of the character itself'.[3] I want to come back to this idea of a 'medium' a little later, too.

Lewes in the *Biographical History* dashes through ideas of the relations of the mind to the outside world, approving the sceptics

---

[1] Ibid Vol. 1
[2] George Eliot *Letters* Vol. 3
[3] George Eliot *Letters* Vol. 4

rather than the idealists, the heroes of inductive thought rather than the metaphysicians. His metaphors for the mind cast light on the centrality to our thought of a pattern of lamps and mirrors (see M. H. Abrams on Romantic aesthetic thought) and through them to the depth of resonance of those metaphors in Eliot's work, particularly in *Middlemarch*. In his description of Bacon, one of his heroes because he originates experiment as the basis of discovery, he quotes Bacon's use of the mirror metaphor in the *Advancement of Learning* when he discusses the idols of the Tribe – the causes of error founded on human nature in general.

'The mind,' Bacon observes, 'is not like a plane mirror, which reflects the images of things exactly as they are; it is like the mirror of an uneven surface, which combines its own figure with the figures of the objects it represents.' And in the *Idols of the Den*, Lewes says, Bacon analyses the errors which spring, not from human nature in general, but from the peculiar character of the individual.

'Besides the causes of error common to all mankind, each individual has his own dark cavern, or den, into which the light is imperfectly admitted, and in the obscurity of which a tutelary idol lurks, at whose shrine the truth is often sacrificed.'[1] If this latter remark recalls vividly all Eliot's imagery of Mr Casaubon, with his blinkered egotism and inadequate learning, pursuing a ghost of an idea into dark caverns and passages with an inadequate candle, the mirror image, *mutatis mutandis*, recalls her great description of Rosamond's self-centred consciousness, rearranging the scratches on a mirror into circles concentric on the light *she casts* on it. When I first came to read George Eliot, criticism concentrated very much on her depictions of great egoists, which I read not in a philosophical sense but purely in a social one, as criticism of unpleasant, self-centred people.

[1] G. H. Lewes *Biographical History of Philosophy* Vol. 3

Reading Lewes's discussions of Kant's, and Fichte's, attempts to form concepts of Duty towards others and the world outside the solipsistic consciousness helps one to understand just what a depth of thought lies behind Eliot's remark, quoted earlier, comparing the concept of Duty to a great central ganglion, or the famous remarks quoted by F. W. H. Myers where she said of the ideas of God, Immortality and Duty how inconceivable was the first, how unbelievable the second, yet how absolute and peremptory the third.

Lewes, in his exposition of Comte's *Philosophy of the Sciences* makes some interesting comments on the conflict, in the higher animals between Personality and Sociality, which he said 'may be denominated *Egoism and Altruism*'. Lewes's account of Comte is a workmanlike summary of his views, from which he himself later diverged, though he retained his belief in positive science as the culmination of human thought. Comte's theories build from the inorganic sciences through organic sciences to human sciences, anatomy, physiology and psychology, moving from there to the social sciences, sociology and social statics, seen as developed through history as Man moved from Theology to Metaphysics to Positive Science. Comte's view is that 'the great social problem' is 'the subjection, as far as possible, of Personality to Sociality, by referring everything to Humanity as a whole'.[1] Lewes argues optimistically that 'Altruism, when energetic, is always found to exercise greater influence on the intelligence than egotism, presenting a larger field for exertion, a more difficult aim, and also a more vigorous demand for its co-operation.'[2] It could be argued – and Lewes himself would no doubt have argued – that this wooden lesson is better learned embodied in a great novel. But both he and Eliot did think very hard in the abstract about the social nature of man as a creature

[1] G. H. Lewes *Comte's Philosophy of the Sciences* (1853)
[2] Ibid.

moving in a social medium, as a cell moves in a physical medium, a Comtean idea.

Other Comtean ideas that Eliot was less enthusiastic about were to do with the place of women. The understanding of the human family as the source of social morality, Comte argued, and Lewes faithfully recorded, meant that the subordination of women was biologically and morally innate.

A just biological philosophy is beginning to discredit those chimerical revolutionary declamations on the pretended equality of the two sexes, by directly demonstrating, either by anatomical investigation, or physiological observation, the radical differences, both physical and moral, which, in all animal species and the human race more especially, so distinctly demarcate them, notwithstanding the preponderance of the specific type.

After completing this scientific examination, Sociology will first prove the radical incompatibility of all social existence with that chimerical 'equality of the sexes' by characterising the special and permanent functions which each must fulfil in the natural economy of the Family. Of the two general attributes which divide Humanity from Animality – intellect and affection – one demonstrates the necessary and inevitable preponderance of the male sex, whilst the other directly characterises the indispensable moderating function devolving on woman independently even of maternal cares, which evidently constitute her sweetest and most important special destination. This invariable economy of the human family never can be really altered unless we suppose a transformation of our cerebral organism.[1]

John Wells has told how, with the leading Positivist, Frederick Harrison on the Committee, the London Library fought a

[1] Ibid

principled battle against women members of it. It has also been argued that Eliot's reluctance to join in the battle for women's education and women's rights wholeheartedly was because of a residual acceptance of the Comtean idea of the radical difference of men from women, even though in a letter she roundly repudiates the 'intention of Nature' argument, 'which is to me a pitiable fallacy. I mean that as a fact of mere zoological evolution, woman seems to have the worst share in existence'.[1] One wonders whether it was Eliot herself whose wit Lewes quotes in *Sea-side Studies* where he records,

> Ungallant physiologists, resting on the evidence of some embryological phenomena, have declared the female to be only *a male in arrested development*; a very impertinent deduction, which was, however, flung back on them by a witty friend of mine, who, hearing that one of her own sex was fond of reading metaphysics and was feared to be suffering from a softened brain, drew her own conclusion as to this masculine course of study, exclaiming '*Man is but woman with a softened brain!*'[2]

I want to end by thinking of Eliot's particular contribution to the novel, in general terms, and in its relation to Lewes's thought. A good place to start might be Lewes's brilliant essay on Dickens, which annoyed Swinburne into castigating it as 'the chattering duncery and the impudent malignity of so consummate and pseudosophical a quack as George Henry Lewes.'[3] Lewes admired Dickens's power and imagination:

> He was a seer of visions; and his visions were of objects at once familiar and potent. Psychologists will understand both the extent and the limitation of the remark, when I

[1] George Eliot *Letters* Vol. 4
[2] G. H. Lewes *Sea-side Studies*
[3] A. C. Swinburne *Charles Dickens* (1913)

say that in no other perfectly sane mind (Blake I believe was not perfectly sane) have I observed vividness of imagination approaching so closely to hallucination.[1]

But his criticism is severe, and implies a contrast with George Eliot.

Only the cultivated who are made fastidious by cultivation paused to consider the pervading commonness of the works, and remarked that they are wholly without glimpses of a nobler life; and that the writer presents an almost unique example of a mind of singular force in which, so to speak, sensations never pass into ideas. Dickens sees and feels, but the logic of feeling seems the only logic he can manage. Thought is strangely absent from his works. I do not suppose a single thoughtful remark on life or character could be found throughout the twenty volumes.[2]

The tone of the beginning of that is unfortunate – but it does point us to the peculiar virtue of George Eliot, the rendering of the passage of sensations into ideas and of ideas seen as immediately as sensations – as she remarks in her great description of Dorothea's passage from egoism to altruism, when she begins to conceive 'with that distinctness which is no longer reflection but feeling – an idea wrought back to the directness of sense like the solidity of objects – that he had an equivalent centre of self, whence the lights and shadows must always fall with a certain difference.'[3] And I should like to add that the ideas that are so embodied again and again in the novels are ideas that Eliot and Lewes, *mutatis mutandis*, shared, about the determined freedom of the individual, and about the human place in a universe of

---

[1] G. H. Lewes 'Dickens in relation to criticism' *Fortnightly Review*. Vol. 17 (Feb 1872)

[2] Ibid

[3] George Eliot *Middlemarch*

which only the egoistic self can see itself as the necessary centre.

Lewes the critic was making this point before George Eliot began to write fiction. Here is his excellent – and very nineteenth-century – definition of Shakespeare's genius as opposed to Goethe's.

Shakespeare's dramas are a beautiful casket of rarities, in which the history of the world passes before our eyes on the invisible thread of time. His plots, to speak according to the ordinary style are no plots, for his plays all turn upon the hidden point (which no philosopher has yet seen and defined) in which the peculiarity of our *ego*, the pretended freedom of our will, clashes with the necessary course of the *whole*.[1]

And by *whole* he means whole play, and also whole society, whole world. In his own comments on how far Goethe was a product of his time and culture he has this to say.

It is profoundly false to say that 'Character is formed by Circumstance' unless the phrase, with unphilosophic equivocation, include the whole complexity of circumstances, from Creation downwards. Character is to outward Circumstance what the Organism is to the outside world: living *in* it, but not specially determined *by* it. A wondrous variety of vegetable and animal organisms live and flourish under circumstances which furnish the *means* of living, but do not determine the *specific forms* of each organism. In the same way *various* characters live under *identical* circumstances, nourished by them, not formed by them. Each character assimilates, from surrounding circumstance, that which by it is assimilable, rejecting the rest. Every biologist knows that Circumstance has a *modifying* influence; but he

[1] G. H. Lewes *Life of Goethe*

also knows that those modifications are only possible within certain limits. Abundance of food and peculiar treatment will modify the ferocity of a wild beast; but it will not make the lion a lamb. I have known a cat, living at a mill, from abundance of fish food take spontaneously to the water; but the cat was distinctively a cat, and not an otter, although she had lost her dread of water.[1]

This idea of the organism living in the world appears in his definition of life itself, in his book on Comte's scientific philosophy. And this passage throws light both on George Eliot's use of Bichat and on her idea of individuals moving in a medium.

Biology is the Science of Life. And first as to the definition of Life. Bichat, unconsciously determined by the ancient prejudice of living bodies being independent of – and antagonistic to – dead bodies . . . gave a definition, which has attained great celebrity, viz.: *'Life is the sum of the functions by which death is resisted'*. Coleridge properly remarks, that he can discover in it, 'no other meaning than that life consists in being able to live' and indeed, if Bichat had only steadily considered the indispensable *co-operation* of the medium (or surrounding circumstances in which an organism is placed) *with* the organism itself, – if he had considered how a slight change in external conditions is sufficient to *revive* a dying animal or to *destroy* a living animal, he would never have propounded such a definition, for he would have seen that so far from organic bodies being independent of external circumstances, they become more and more dependent on them as their organisation becomes higher, so that *organism* and *a medium* are the two correlative ideas of life; while inversely, it is in proportion as we *descend* the scale till we arrive at the most universal of all phenomena – those

[1] G. H. Lewes *Life of Goethe*

of gravitation, that the independence of a surrounding medium is manifested.[1]

Compare, among many possible passages, the end of *Middlemarch*, about Dorothea –

Certainly, those determining acts of her life were not idealy beautiful. They were the mixed results of young and noble impulse struggling amidst the conditions of an imperfect social state in which great feelings will often take the aspect of error, and great faith the aspect of illusion. For there is no creature whose inward being is so strong that it is not greatly determined by what lies outside it.[2]

It is a commonplace that Victorian thought – evolution, religious doubt, biology, industrialism – moved Man from the centre of things in the way he had been moved by the Copernican revolution. Lewes and Eliot were conscious that the world was not made for human beings, who were creatures – or if we want to do away with the idea of a Creator – organisms in it. Lewes has an eloquent passage in the Comte book of the idea that Man is the Measure of all things. He repudiates gods made in human images, and later ideas that human Reason is an adequate instrument for measuring and comprehending Divine Law. God does not correspond to human intelligence, as it does not feel human passion. He ends rhapsodically nevertheless with an endorsement of Mystery, and unlike the hero of Tennyson's *Maud*, who saw the stars as 'innumerable pitiless fires that burn and brand/ His Nothingness into man', Lewes still wishes to say with the psalmist, 'The heavens declare the Glory of God'. The complexity and vastness of the world is both daunting and challenging and exciting.

Eliot wrote to Sara Hennell from her seaside studies:

[1] G. H. Lewes *Comte's Philosophy of the Sciences*
[2] George Eliot *Middlemarch*

I quite approve of your disinterring that strange beast but I really give the preference to the wonderful Cydippes that we found yesterday floating on the sunny sea – tiny crystal globes with delicate *meridians* of cilia, and long streamers spreading behind them as they float. I feel everyday a greater disinclination for theories and arguments about the origin of things in the presence of all this mystery and beauty and pain and ugliness, that floods one with conflicting emotions.[1]

She then refers to a recent article by Herbert Spencer, with whom we began, and who was, the London Librarian assures me, as a committee member of the library, responsible for the now mythic statement that all fiction but Eliot's should be excluded, as hers was philosophy. Spencer says:

After all that has been said, the ultimate mystery of things remains just as it was. The sincere man of science, content fearlessly to follow wherever the evidence leads him, becomes by each new inquiry more profoundly convinced that the Universe is an insoluble problem . . . He learns at once the greatness and the littleness of human intellect . . . He alone *knows* that under all things there lies an impenetrable mystery.[2]

And if we think Lewes's prescription of 'thoughtful remarks on life or character' in novels is a little dull or heavy, consider this, from *Middlemarch*:

That element of tragedy which lies in the very fact of frequency has not yet wrought itself into the coarse emotion of mankind; and perhaps our frames could hardly bear much of it. If we had a keen vision and feeling of all ordinary

---

[1] George Eliot *Letters* Vol. 2
[2] Spencer's article was in the *Westminster Review* Vol. 67 (April 1857)

human life, it would be like hearing the grass grow and the squirrel's heart beat, and we should die of that roar which lies on the other side of silence.[1]

The comparisons with plants and animals – as in the earlier more savagely comic moment in *Adam Bede* when Adam tries to interest Hetty in an ant carrying a caterpillar, and the little mirror-obsessed egoist cannot be interested – make human beings, and novels, more, not less important. A good place to end might be where Lewes, in *Sea-side Studies*, thinks his way back from the marvels of the world which is not ourselves to the marvels of libraries, of the London Library which he has already mentioned. He is musing excitedly on the 'convoluted bands' to be discerned in Actiniae, or sea-anemones.

> Moreover the first step in organology must be to determine whether the *product* of the organ is present, e.g. ova in ovaries, bile in liver, urea in kidneys and so on; and until chemical reagents have detected urea or bile in those convoluted bands, we may rest on the assurance that these bands are neither urinary nor biliary organs. To look for such special organs in so simple an organism, seems to me like seeking for a circulating library in an Esquimaux village.
>
> The mention of a library carries my thought, by an easy transition, to our evening studies, when the labours of the day are over, the microscope is put up, the work-table is quitted, and the delicious calm of candlelight invites us to quiet intercourse with one of the great spirits of the past, or one of their worthy successors in the present. It is well thus to refresh the mind with Literature. Contact with Nature, and her inexhaustible wealth, is apt to beget an impatience at man's achievements; and there is danger of the mind becoming so immersed in details, so strained to

[1] George Eliot *Middlemarch*

contemplation of the physical glories of the Universe, as to forget the higher grandeurs of the soul, the nobler beauties of the moral universe. From this danger we are saved by the thrill of a fine poem, the swelling sympathy with a noble thought, which flood the mind anew with a sense of man's greatness, and the greatness of his aspirations. It is not wise to dwarf Man by comparisons with Nature; only when he grows presumptuous, may we teach him modesty by pointing to her grandeur. At other times it is well to keep before us our high calling and our high estate. Literature, in its finest moods, does this. And when I think of the delight given by every true book to generations after generations, moulding souls and humanising savage impetuosities, exalting hopes and prompting nobles deeds, I vary the poet's phrase and exclaim 'An honest book's the noblest work of man'.[1]

[1] G. H. Lewes *Sea-side Studies*

RUDYARD KIPLING

1865–1936

JOHN JULIUS NORWICH

RUDYARD KIPLING

'How far is St Helena from a little child at play?'
What makes you want to wander there with all the world
                                                    between?
Oh, Mother, call your son again or else he'll run away.
(*No one thinks of winter when the grass is green!*)

'How far is St Helena from a fight in Paris Street?'
I haven't time to answer now – the men are falling fast.
The guns begin to thunder, and the drums begin to beat.
(*If you take the first step, you will take the last!*)

'How far is St Helena from the field of Austerlitz?'
You couldn't hear me if I told – so loud the cannon roar.
But not so far for people who are living by their wits.
('*Gay go up*' means '*Gay go down*' the wide world o'er!)

'How far is St Helena from an Emperor of France?'
I cannot see – I cannot tell – the Crowns they dazzle so.
The Kings sit down to dinner, and the Queens stand up to
                                                    dance.
(*After open weather you may look for snow!*)

'How far is St Helena from the Capes of Trafalgar?'
A longish way – a longish way – with ten year more to run.

It's South across the water underneath a falling star.
(*What you cannot finish you must leave undone!*)

'How far is St Helena from the Beresina ice?'
An ill way – a chill way – the ice begins to crack.
But not so far for gentlemen who never took advice.
(*When you can't go forward you must e'en come back!*)

'How far is St Helena from the field of Waterloo?'
A near way – a clear way – the ship will take you soon.
A pleasant place for gentlemen with little left to do.
(*Morning never tries you till the afternoon!*)

'How far from St Helena to the Gate of Heaven's Grace?'
That no one knows – that no one knows – and no one ever
will.
But fold your hands across your heart and cover up your
face,
And after all your trapesings, child, lie still!

I T   W A S   T H A T   P O E M, more than any other of his writings, that introduced me to Rudyard Kipling. My parents had read me *The Just-So Stories* and, I think, at least one of *The Jungle Books*; but these had got confused in my infant mind with all the other animal stories that are part and parcel of an English childhood, and never really made the same sort of impression on me as Alice or even Dr Dolittle. *A St Helena Lullaby* was different. My father would recite it to himself while shaving in the morning, and occasionally again in the evening after dinner. I loved it from the first time I heard it, and it was the first poem of Kipling's that I ever learnt by heart. Field-Marshal Wavell, including it in his anthology *Other Men's Flowers*, expresses surprise that the poet got the chronological order wrong, Trafalgar having in fact been fought six weeks before Austerlitz; but Kipling, I am sure, knew this perfectly well. For him, the dramatic order was far more important than the chronological. The point was that Trafalgar was a defeat: he could hardly introduce it while he was still tracing the rise of Napoleon's career.

The poem is Kipling through and through. No other poet, I suspect, in all English literary history would have chosen so artificial a formula for each verse – question, answer, elaboration of answer, monitory aphorism – and brought it off so triumphantly. We can recognise that faultless ear, that ability to combine as no-one else could the occasional shaft of pure poetry (like those opening words 'How far is St Helena') with the easy rhythms of everyday colloquial speech; the unfailing instinct for what is precisely the right word, as in 'trapesings'; the strong moral undercurrent that is such a Kipling trademark; and just that little hint of patronising archness that is, so regrettably, another. Finally, am I alone in believing that I can trace, as in so many other poems by the same hand, a faint echo of the Victorian Music Hall? In Napoleon's day the Music Hall had not yet been invented; but if it had, and if the Lullaby had been set to a good, catchy tune, would audiences not have taken it to their hearts in the same way as they were later to do with similarly belittling songs about Kruger, or Kaiser Bill, or even, in our own day, Hitler?

And yet, although the poem could in one sense have been written by no-one other than Kipling, in another it is not at all typical of him. With his deeply implanted mistrust of democracy and his admiration for what he used to describe as 'the strong man governing alone', we might have expected him to make Napoleon one of his heroes, just as he idolised Mussolini – and would probably have idolised Hitler too if his lifelong hatred of Germany had not most fortunately prevented his doing so. In fact, his feelings about Napoleon were probably much the same as those which had impelled the furious Beethoven to strike out the dedication of the Eroica Symphony: disappointment and disillusion at the sight of a brilliant young general – who might have saved and restored prosperity to his country – returning it instead, his head turned by early success and his own monstrous ambition, to the demoralisation and disgrace from which he had rescued it only twenty years before. Napoleon was a genius, and a thoroughgoing professional – two qualities Kipling admired above all others; but he was also an adventurer who prostituted his immense talents for his own glory – and that was not to be forgiven.

But did not Kipling do the same? Did not he, too, sacrifice his prodigious natural gifts on the altar of vulgarity and violence, abandoning the lyricism of which he was so obviously capable – and which could have made him the successor to Tennyson – in favour of slangy doggerel, false heartiness, provincial journalese, the songs of the Music Hall and – worst of all perhaps – the mangled and mutilated language in which he attempted to reproduce the dialect of the lower classes, with results, as George Orwell put it, as embarrassing as the humorous recitation at a church social? Many contemporary critics believed that he did – among them Max Beerbohm, who saw him as nothing more than 'a Bank Holiday cornet virtuoso on the spree'.

It wasn't often that Max missed the point; but this time he missed it totally – and perhaps that is not altogether surprising. Max was an aesthete, an exquisite, a Yellow Book man: his soul was as different from Kipling's as any man's soul could possibly be. His fastidious distaste for the brash rum-ti-tum of *Barrack-Room Ballads* and the regimental crudities of *Soldiers Three* blinded him not only to the fact that this rather unpleasant young man had given the ordinary British soldier a voice – something that no writer had ever done before – but also to his extraordinary literary talents: his unerring way with words, his boundless intellectual curiosity and powers of observation – powers so sensitive it sometimes seems that not only his mind but every one of his senses possesses its own separate set of antennae, responding almost psychically to the world around him.

And many other people since Max have made the same mistake – that of judging this most varied and wide-ranging of writers on the strength of the more objectionable aspects of his work alone: if not the crudity and the brashness, then the right-wing prejudices, the suggestions of anti-semitism (though these are mild compared with those of his contemporaries Belloc and Chesterton), the shameless reflection of what tends nowadays to be considered as British imperialism at its worst. In all these areas Kipling lays himself almost masochistically open to attack – as he does, too, in another, more surprising, characteristic of his: his simplicity. In virtually all his poetry and in all his short stories except a few in the last two collections – *Debits and Credits* and *Limits and Renewals* – he is immediately and transparently comprehensible. Usually, as T. S. Eliot pointed out in his celebrated introduction to his choice of Kipling's verse, we find ourselves defending contemporary writers against accusations of obscurity; with Kipling, on the other hand, the charge is more often that of excessive lucidity. People, he goes on, may be exasperated by poetry that they can't understand; but they also tend to be contemptuous of poetry they understand too easily. Kipling's fault is not intellectual arrogance; what many of his critics, whether they admit it or not, find hardest to forgive is the way he appeals to the commonest collective emotions.

Now this may be true enough as far as it goes; unfortunately, it does not go anywhere near far enough. Kipling stands arraigned on several other charges too, a good deal more serious than that of simplicity or those which concern his political opinions. Politics are, after all, ephemeral; today's news is tomorrow's history. Besides, most intelligent people find their political views changing and developing as they grow older, and Kipling was no exception. The point is – thank God – that he was never a professional politician. He was – first, last and always – a writer, and it is as a writer that he must be judged.

Technically, there is no doubt, he was superb. Equally at ease with verse or prose, he had an instinct for the rhythms of the English language that might have been the envy of many writers far greater than he, together with a gift for the telling phrase unequalled by any other writer since Shakespeare. George Orwell has listed several that have passed into the language: 'East is East and West is West'; 'The White Man's Burden'; 'What do they know of England who only England know?'; 'The Female of the Species is more deadly than the Male'; 'Somewhere East of Suez'; and 'Paying the Dane-geld'. I would add 'The Law of the Jungle'; 'The Tumult and the Shouting Dies'; 'The Colonel's Lady and Judy O'Grady' and even, perhaps, 'The Glory of the Garden'. And all this he combined with a fertility of imagination that sometimes takes one's breath away. How many writers would be capable, even if they wished to do so, of devoting a short story – and not in any sense a children's story either – to a detailed description of a polo match, seen from the point of view of the ponies? Kipling did it in 1895 with *The Maltese Cat*, and brought it off triumphantly and without a trace of archness; moreover his horses are real horses, not *Animal Farm*-type symbols for human beings. Three years later, in *The Ship that Found Herself*, he went further still and made the various parts of the ship the chief characters, while in *.007* he did the same thing with a railway engine; I shall be giving you an example later. Thanks to his early journalistic training he wrote, throughout his life, quickly, efficiently and concisely; and though his taste frequently let him down, his technique hardly ever did.

His weaknesses – and they are many and grave – seem to me to be principally psychological; and to understand them properly we must go back to his formative years, and to the several major traumas of his life, all of which left deep scars and from none of which he ever entirely recovered. The first was his and his sister's enforced return from India when he was six, and their farming

84

out with the infamous Mr and Mrs Holloway in Southsea. It was not just the severity and lovelessness of this household, the ill-treatment inflicted on both the children (but particularly Rudyard) by the woman they were obliged to call 'Aunt Rosa' and the cruel bullying of him by the Holloways' considerably older son that led him to refer to the place, on the rare occasions when he could be persuaded to talk about it, as the 'House of Desolation'; it was above all the feeling of betrayal. How could his parents, whom he loved and whom he believed to love him, have abandoned him and his sister so heartlessly, entrusting them without a second thought to a wicked step-mother straight out of a fairy tale? The nightmare was to last a full five years – until Alice Kipling returned to England to see her children, went upstairs to kiss her son goodnight and saw him instinctively raise his arm to ward off an expected blow. Then and only then was she to take them away; but the damage had been done.

Three times over Kipling tells us the story of life with the Holloways: first in his short story *Baa, Baa, Black Sheep* (written eleven years later after his return to India and one of few occasions in his work, as Edmund Wilson has pointed out, where he sympathises with the victims rather than the instigators of a severely repressive discipline), next – with a few minor alterations made necessary by the plot – in his early and extremely bad novel *The Light that Failed*, and finally, at the end of his life, in his posthumously-published autobiography *Something of Myself*. In the first two, at least, he was not on oath: did he exaggerate his miseries? The answer seems to be that he did not. His sister, Mrs John Fleming, told his first biographer Lord Birkenhead that she and her brother never discussed those Southsea days: 'they hurt too much'; and forty-three years after their departure his wife recorded in her diary: 'Rud takes me to see Lorne Lodge . . . where he was so misused and forlorn and desperately unhappy as a child, and talks of it all with horror.'

In *Something of Myself*, Kipling writes that the experience had left him 'drained. . . . of any capacity for real, personal hate for the rest of [his] days'; but his work, together with what we know of his character, scarcely bears this out. I believe he came a good deal closer to the truth when he wrote towards the end of *Baa, Baa, Black Sheep*: 'When young lips have drunk deep of the bitter waters of Hate, Suspicion, and Despair, all the Love in the world will not wholly take away that knowledge; though it may turn darkened eyes for a while to the light, and teach Faith where no Faith was'. That same desperate insecurity that had caused him instinctively to ward off his mother's kiss was to remain with him always, ineffectually hidden behind the interminable bluster and bragadoccio. So too was his extraordinary secretiveness, his hatred of interviews and almost pathological fear of journalists, despite having been such an inspired one himself. For those who are hunted or persecuted – and Kipling at Southsea was unquestionably both – self-revelation means destruction. Keep yourself to yourself: or, as he was later to put it:

> Unless you come of the gypsy stock
>   That steals by night and day
> Lock your heart with a double lock
>   And throw the key away.

Anyone reading his so-called autobiography – which was, incidentally, suggested as a form of therapy by his doctor – will see how faithfully this precept was observed.

Kipling's next stage, the United Services College at Westward Ho!, was an immense improvement on Southsea; but if we are to judge from the picture Kipling gives of it in *Stalky & Co.* – I say 'if', because the originals of his two principal characters have published very different accounts of the place – it still seems to have embodied all that was worst in the English Public School system of High Victorian days. I shall pass over it quickly, if only because I have always found the book almost unreadable

in its persistent obsession with persecution, bullying and flog-
ging, to say nothing of its muddled thinking. As in *Kim*, Kipling
never seems quite sure which side he is on. First he enlists our
sympathies for the boys' rebellion against their sadistic masters;
then he explains that all the beatings and canings are necessary
for one of his favourite processes, described all too frequently
throughout his work as 'licking the cubs into shape', to make
them capable of governing the Empire. The final scene of the
story entitled *A Little Prep.*, in which the Head undertakes personally to flog the whole school, while the boys stand round him
cheering, is little short of grotesque.

Did Kipling swallow the public school ethos? Up to a point,
yes: the dreadful heartiness of *Stalky & Co.* tells its own story.
Worse, his later epistolary style – in which, among countless
other infelicities, he invariably refers to his meals as 'grub' and
seldom fails to replace the 'th' in 'them' with an apostrophe –
shows that, unlike most men of his time, he never grew out of
it. On the other hand he never swallowed it altogether. Though
that inspired reference to 'the flannelled fools at the wicket, and
the muddied oafs at the goals' was still four years in the future, he
made no secret of despising all games except polo – his extreme
short-sightedness may have had something to do with it – and
spent every spare moment of leisure reading and writing: some
of his schoolboy verses are already quite astonishingly assured.
Browning and Poe, Swinburne and Ruskin – in literature at
least, he was a good deal less of a philistine than he pretended,
and his later critics believed. He read French fluently – he had
fallen in love with the country after having been taken there by
his father at the age of twelve to see the great Paris Exhibition
of 1878 – and, so far as we can understand, Latin: he certainly
had a passion for Horace, keeping an annotated copy of the
Odes at his bedside. For all its shortcomings, the United Services
College had done him proud; and by the age of seventeen he
was ready to enter the next chapter of his life: his return to India

and his seven years as a working journalist for the *Civil and Military Gazette*, Lahore.

It was, one suspects, his happiest time:

We shall go back to the boltless doors,
　To the life unaltered our childhood knew –
To the naked feet on the cool, dark floors,
　And the high-ceiled rooms that the Trade blows through:

To the trumpet-flowers and the moon beyond,
　And the tree-toads' chorus drowning all –
And the lisp of the split banana-frond
　That talked us to sleep when we were small.

Already – thanks to his early childhood – speaking fluent Hindustani, unshackled by the discipline of the army or the Indian Civil Service, he could mix in every *milieu*, study every society, from the tea-table of the hopeful English girls – known locally as 'the fishing fleet' – newly arrived in Delhi and Simla, to the earthiness of the barrack-room and the exoticism of the bazaar. Thus it was that by 1886 there suddenly appeared the first writer of real stature that British India had ever produced: an overworked young man of twenty-one, filling the vacant spaces of his newspaper with short stories and satirical verses that instantly made his name a household word the length and breadth of India – and, a year or two later, of England too. They impressed not only by their originality – no-one had ever attempted anything of the kind before – and the brilliance of the writing, but also by their sheer quantity: by the time he left India in 1889 at the age of twenty-four Kipling had produced – not counting the two books which he wrote with other members of his family – no less than nine volumes of poetry and prose. Two years later, by the end of 1891, the number had risen to sixteen.

So it was that when Kipling arrived in London, by way of

America, in 1889, he was already a celebrity. Not all the *litterati* shared Max Beerbohm's opinions. Vulgar and tasteless he might be; yet 'who else', asked George Moore, 'except Whitman, has written with the whole language since the Elizabethans?' Edmund Gosse confessed to 'a peculiar thrill'; Henry James described him, as only Henry James could, as 'a strangely clever youth who has stolen the formidable mask of maturity and rushes about making people jump with the deep sounds that issue from its painted lips'. True, there were to be disappointments: *The Light that Failed*, which was published at the end of 1890, caused many critics to opine that young Mr Kipling, though an undoubted master of the short story, was incapable of writing a good novel. As it happened, they were quite right; yet his star continued to rise, and only two years later, James went further still. 'Kipling strikes me personally,' he wrote, 'as the most complete man of genius . . . that I have ever known.' Kipling's vanity must have been flattered by the acclaim; but he showed little gratitude, or even appreciation. From the beginning he seems to have felt himself an outsider, and no wonder. This, after all, was *fin-de-siècle* London, the London of Moore and Meredith, of Aubrey Beardsley and Oscar Wilde; in the world of art, of his own uncles Poynter and Burne-Jones. It might admire him as the curious, exotic phenomenon he was; but its values could never be his values, it could never take him to its heart. Nor did he wish it to. This strange, hypersophisticated society in which he suddenly found himself must have seemed languid, self-satisfied and more than a little decadent:

> But I consort with long-haired things
> In velvet collar-rolls,
> Who talk about the Aims of Art,
> And 'theories' and 'goals',
> And moo and coo with women-folk
> About their blessed souls.

Such people were, he found, sublimely uninterested in the vast, many-faceted and infinitely more exciting world outside. He sensed their enmity and retreated, as he was so often to do in the future, into his shell. Invitations were curtly refused. What had begun as suspicion turned first to dislike, and eventually to contempt. No wonder he didn't stay in London long.

In January 1892 he married his American wife Caroline, sister of a young publisher named Wolcott Balestier who had, in his own way, taken the literary world by storm at about the same time. More impressively, he had managed to penetrate Kipling's formidable defences as few others had done. Recent suggestions that their friendship had homosexual overtones strike me as wildly improbable to say the least; Kipling was certainly pros-trated when Wolcott died of typhoid in 1891, but this was always his reaction to the deaths of those he loved or admired – after the death of Robert Louis Stevenson, whom he had never met, Lord Birkenhead tells us that he could not write a line for three weeks – and his marriage can probably be attributed less to any wish of preserving the association with his friend's family than to the determination of Carrie herself, who was effortlessly to dominate her husband, for all his transparent *machismo*, for the next forty-four years until his death.

A fortnight after their marriage they left London for America, Canada and Japan – they were always compulsive travellers – before settling in August on the Balestier property at Brattle-boro, Connecticut. At first they were happy enough: it was here that Kipling produced for his children the two *Jungle Books* and several of the enchanting *Just-So Stories*, works which are alone enough to rank him second only to Lewis Carroll among the greatest children's writers in English. *The Just-So Stories*, which were to be published only in 1902, are obviously intended for very young children and are straightforward enough; *The Jungle Books*, on the other hand, tell us as much about Kipling as anything that he ever wrote.

Nowadays, the phrase 'The Law of the Jungle' – one of those catchphrases of his that have passed into the language – has a very different connotation from that which he intended. We use it today to mean, roughly speaking, anarchy; for Kipling, it signified precisely the opposite. *The Jungle Books* are in fact shot through with his instinctive imperialism, his love of an imposed order, without which countries and peoples would, he believed, lapse into that chaos which he dreaded more than anything else in the world. From the very first page we find Mowgli undergoing that favourite process of Kipling's that I have already mentioned, the process that he liked to describe as 'being licked into shape'. In this case the little Indian boy who has been adopted by the beasts is being *taught* the Law of the Jungle, that inflexible code of conduct which all the animals except the monkeys know by instinct, and which makes this primeval world the happy, curiously well-ordered place it is. Yet for Kipling, even this natural law is not enough: it is no coincidence that Mowgli – true to his origins, for he is after all a superior being – grows up to be a Forest Ranger and a servant of the Raj, providing a striking parallel with Kim, as we shall see.

The first American years were happy ones for the Kiplings; trouble, however, came all too soon – when they ran foul of Carrie's mildly disreputable brother Beatty Balestier. There is no doubt that they had right on their side; on the other hand they had already antagonised a good many of their neighbours by what were considered their stuck-up English ways, and as relations between the two parties deteriorated Kipling could hardly have played his hand worse. The affair reached its climax at a legal hearing in May 1896, when, under cross-examination, he contradicted himself again and again and made himself little less than a laughing-stock. It was the greatest humiliation of his life. Soon afterwards he and Carrie left Connecticut for ever.

But their greatest American tragedy was still to come. Three years later they sailed with their three young children for New

York, and on their arrival were all five of them stricken with
influenza. Kipling's turned almost at once to pneumonia, and
for a week he hung between life and death; only after he was
well on the road to recovery did his wife dare to break it to him
that their six-year-old daughter Josephine had died of the same
virus a few days before. Here was another blow that he never
fully overcame. After they returned to their English home at
Rottingdean he wrote to his mother that he saw her everywhere,
every time a door was opened, in every green corner of the
garden. Her name could not be mentioned in his presence: only
in his poetry – and, it must be said, in some of his most embarrassing poetry – could he express something of what he felt:

> Her brows are bound with bracken-fronds,
> And golden elf-locks fly above
> Her eyes as bright as diamonds
> And bluer than the sky above.
>
> In moccasins and deer-skin cloak,
> Unfearing, free and fair she flits,
> And lights her little damp-wood smoke
> To show her Daddy where she flits.
>
> For far – oh, very far behind,
> So far she cannot call to him,
> Comes Tegumai alone to find
> The daughter that was all to him!

There was to be only one further tragedy in Kipling's life: the
death in the First World War of his son John, at the age of seventeen. Here his grief was almost certainly compounded by feelings
of desperate guilt, knowing as he did that John, whose eyesight
was as bad as his own, had been rejected for the army on medical
grounds and had obtained his commission only after his father
had made a personal appeal to his old friend Lord Roberts of

Kandahar. He dealt with it, as he had with Josephine, by ruthlessly eliminating everything that could remind him of the child he had lost – a reaction with which many of us would, I think, find difficult to sympathise, and which demonstrates once again Kipling's strange inability to face up to personal adversity. Even so, he seems to have been less haunted by John than he was by Josephine; his magnificent later work for the Imperial War Graves Commission may well have provided comfort of a kind that he could never have known after the loss of his little daughter.

The beginning of the twentieth century found Kipling entering the middle period of his life. He was rich, he was famous. His recent illness had made the headlines everywhere; telegrams had poured in from all over the world. In 1900, too, he completed the book on which he had been working for the past two years and which was to prove his greatest prose masterpiece – the only really satisfactory full-length work, in fact, that he ever wrote and, in the opinion of Mr Nirad C. Chaudhuri (no mean authority, as you will agree), the best book on India ever written. Certainly no-one else, British or Indian, before or since, has written of India in quite the same way, embracing in a single universal vision all its classes and castes and religions. Moreover, he writes with love – the love that he acquired from his Indian childhood and that he never lost. Neither is there, at this stage of Kipling's development, any suggestion of racial superiority. To him, British culture was superior to Indian only because the British were the stronger, and happened to be better at the arts of administration and government. In *Kim*, as in nearly all his Indian stories, the natives are infinitely more sympathetic, and often a good deal wiser, than the British, while Christian missionaries come off worst of all.

Herein lies the value of *Kim*. The travellers and the unending commerce of the Grand Trunk Road live again in its pages; the characters – the horse-dealer Mahboub Ali, the rich old widow in her bullock-cart, the sinister jeweller Lurgan Sahib and of course the Lama himself, are as fully-rounded and as unforgettable as those of Dickens – though, like Dickens, one feels that Kipling sometimes has a little trouble breathing life into his protagonist: compared with his friends and associates on the Road, Kim himself tends to emerge as a surprisingly misty figure. No matter: with so exotic and colourful a pageant passing ceaselessly before our eyes, we hardly notice. For *Kim* is a panorama, set against the eternal backdrop of the Himalayas and the more transitory one of what, thanks once again to Kipling, we have come to call The Great Game.

But panoramas are not novels, and it is as a novel that the book ultimately fails. First of all, it is picaresque: more a collection of linked short stories than a novel in the true sense of the word. But there is more to the problem than that. Its real weakness was, I think, first identified by Edmund Wilson, who pointed out that the fundamental conflict from which the plot derives its interest actually comes to nothing: the two forces – India and the British Raj – never really engage. Throughout the book we are left in no doubt which of the two is closer to Kim's own heart: we admire – indeed, we are fascinated by – his ability to merge into the life of India as he instantly does the moment the school holidays begin, and we naturally expect that, sooner or later, he will find himself torn between the two allegiances. But nothing of the kind occurs. At the end of the book, what happens? Just as Mowgli became a Forest Ranger, Kim finally emerges as the Sahib he is and gains promotion in the Secret Service. Thus, as in *Stalky*, sympathy for the weaker of the two forces (India) gives way to glorification of the stronger (the Raj). Despite a clear basic conflict, Kipling has once again – as he always did – avoided any direct confrontation between the two sides.

Where Wilson surely goes too far is when he argues that 'it never seems to occur to his creator that [Kim's decision] constitutes a betrayal of the Lama'; Kipling would have retorted that it was nothing of the sort, that Kim's course and the Lama's ran, not contrary to each other, but parallel. He would probably have gone on to explain that Kim could not have acted otherwise than he did: he would have known, like any other sensible person, that British rule was the best thing – not necessarily for Britain, but for India; that India needed a firm hand; that the British were good rulers, most of the Indian Civil Service being kind, competent, selfless and incorruptible; and, finally, that if the British were to leave there would be bloodshed on a huge and hideous scale. (How right he was.)

And this brings us to one of the most fundamental tenets of Kipling's imperialist philosophy: the concept of the Empire as duty, based not on what can be got out of the subject peoples but on what can be contributed to their education and welfare. He illustrated it best in the appeal he addressed to the Americans, after the brief Spanish-American War of 1898 left them the somewhat embarrassed masters of Cuba and the Philippines:

Take up the White Man's burden –
    Send forth the best ye breed –
Go, bind your sons to exile
    To serve your captives' need;
To wait in heavy harness
    On fluttered folk and wild –
Your new-caught, sullen peoples,
    Half-devil and half-child.

And note, please, that marvellous word 'fluttered'. Could anyone but Kipling have used it? I don't think so.

The appearance of *Kim* coincided almost exactly with the outbreak of the Boer War. Kipling flung himself into the cause heart and soul. Not only were the Boers rebels: their attitude to the black Africans was precisely that which he most deplored. Besides, the war provided him with just the excitement and activity that he needed after his family tragedy. He travelled ceaselessly backwards and forwards to South Africa, writing, lecturing, reporting – and, incidentally, getting his first – and virtually his last – experience of battle. It was a small, inconclusive engagement to which he was driven by a native driver in a bullock cart – all his life he was terrified of horses – and it is unlikely that his life was ever very seriously at risk; but it thrilled him to the core and enabled him, he felt, to write still more graphically of the army in the field.

And so, in a way, he did; but he was no longer the Kipling of the early Indian stories. The first major war that his country had fought in his lifetime seems somehow to have desensitised him, even coarsened him. His imperialism, imbued with a new ferocity, is no longer tempered with the same admiration, even the same sympathy and understanding, for the subject peoples. Gunga Din was no longer a better man than he was. He would never write another *Kim*. Henceforth he was a member of the Establishment. He would never hesitate to criticise the Government, the generals, above all the politicians – a race he professed to loathe – including even his own cousin Stanley Baldwin, whose moderately enlightened policies towards India and Ireland he saw as dragging his country further and further down the slippery path to socialism. But the rightness of the cause would never again be in doubt.

It comes even now as something of a surprise to read that Kipling's ideal of manliness as immortalised in *If* – probably the most famous of all his poems – was based on the character of that most pig-headed of men Sir Leander Starr Jameson, leader of the Jameson Raid of December 1895 and one of those principally responsible for the outbreak of hostilities less than four years later. Jameson had received no less than six messages to the effect that the British in Johannesburg would not rise in support of his projected armed raid into the Transvaal, but he went in anyway. The result of this ludicrous decision was sixty-five out of 600 of his own men killed and wounded, the Boers losing just one. Jameson's final humiliation was to be sent back to London by President Kruger and to be sentenced to fifteen months' imprisonment in Holloway prison. No wonder that a friend of mine used to keep, framed above his desk, an inscription reading, 'If you can keep your head when all about you / Are losing theirs and blaming it on you – could it be that you have incorrectly appraised the situation?'

It was just as well, when the war finally ended, that Kipling found a new interest – one which was to occupy his creative energies almost as obsessively as India had done twenty years before: this was England, which he liked to refer to as 'my favourite foreign country', and in particular English history. In 1902 he and Carrie left Rottingdean – long since made intolerable by autograph hunters – and settled at Bateman's, an old and gloomy mill protected by thirty-three acres of farmland near Burwash in Sussex. With his usual thoroughness, he spent days and weeks in the local Records Office, immersing himself in Sussex history and legend; and the result was two children's books, *Puck of Pook's Hill* – published in 1906 – and *Rewards and Fairies*, which appeared four years later.

I call them 'children's books' only with some hesitation: Kipling himself described them somewhat differently, as stories intended to be read by children 'before people realised that they were meant for grown-ups', and several of the stories in *Rewards and Fairies* are so heavy with unstated implication and symbolism as to constitute something of a challenge to the maturest adult; essentially, however, children's books is what they are. Kipling, as we have seen, was no stranger to the genre. Now that his children were growing up, they needed something more immediately relevant to their own lives than *Just-So Stories* and *Jungle Books*. These new stories, however, were nothing like the textbooks that they might have used at school; for they were designed not so much to teach their young readers English history as to impress upon them the 2000-year continuity of life on this island, the ability of its people to draw strength from the eternal land itself and thus to survive war and adversity.

This theme was to emerge as one of the principal *leitmotifs* of Kipling's later work, a theme which was to run through some of his prose and a good deal of his poetry for the rest of his life. He was never, in any real sense of the word, a historian; he saw history much more as a journalist would, combining the long, broad sweep with an infallible eye for the significant detail and that characteristic gift – which we notice, too, in his Indian stories – of seeing great events through the eyes of a single not very important individual. And of course he remained an imperialist – which is why, time and time again, he reverts to one of his favourite subjects: England under the Roman occupation. Let me give you one of many examples of the way he combines the two, in *The Roman Centurion's Song*:

Legate, I had the news last night – my cohort ordered home
By ship to Portus Itius and thence by road to Rome.
I've marched the companies aboard, the arms are stowed
below:
Now let another take my sword. Command me not to go!

I've served in Britain forty years, from Vectis to the Wall.
I have none other home than this, nor any life at all.
Last night I did not understand, but, now the hour draws
near
That calls me to my native land, I feel that land is here.

Here where men say my name was made, here where my
work was done;
Here where my dearest dead are laid – my wife – my wife
and son;
Here where time, custom, grief and toil, age, memory,
service, love,

Have rooted me in British soil. Ah, how can I remove?

For me this land, that sea, these airs, those folk and fields
suffice.
What purple Southern pomp can match our changeful
Northern skies,
Black with December snows unshed or pearled with August
haze –
The clanging arch of steel-grey March, or June's
long-lighted days?

You'll follow widening Rhodanus till vine and olive lean
Aslant before the sunny breeze that sweeps Nemausus clean
To Arelate's triple gate; but let me linger on,
Here where our stiff-necked British oaks confront
Euroclydon!

You'll take the old Aurelian Road through shore-descending
pines
Where, blue as any peacock's neck, the Tyrrhene Ocean
shines.
You'll go where laurel crowns are won, but – will you e'er
forget
The scent of hawthorn in the sun, or bracken in the wet?

Let me work here for Britain's sake – at any task you will –
A marsh to drain, a road to make or native troops to drill.
Some Western camp (I know the Pict) or granite Border
keep,
Mid seas of heather derelict, where our old messmates sleep.

Legate, I come to you in tears – My cohort ordered home!
I've served in Britain forty years. What should I do in Rome?

Here is my heart, my soul, my mind – the only life I know.
I cannot leave it all behind. Command me not to go!

'Command' – that's the word: not 'allow' or 'permit'. Here is a centurion whose long service has licked him thoroughly into shape. He is not demanding any rights or asking any favours. What he understands is obedience. Only a command will do. And this brings us to another secret of Kipling's strength: his ability to think himself into the mind, not just of a a professional soldier, but of any working man. Work – the things a man does for a living, the objects that surround him, the tools he uses, even the technical language with which he describes all these things – never cease to fascinate him and provide a theme for much of his later writing. Take this passage, for example, from his short story *.007*:

> He was pushed forward a foot at a time, whirled backwards, his rear drivers clinking and clanking, a quarter of a mile; jerked into a switch . . . bunted into a Red D, or Merchant's Transport car and, with no knowledge of the weight behind him, started up anew. . . . Then he would wait a few minutes, watching the whirled lanterns, deafened with the clang of the bells, giddy with the vision of sliding cars, his brake-pump panting forty to the minute, his front coupler lying sideways on his cow-catcher, like a tired dog's tongue in his mouth, and the whole of him covered with half-burnt coal-dust.

Or, from his poem *McAndrew's Hymn*, lines like these:

> The crank-throws give the double-bass, the feed-pump sobs
> an' heaves,
> An' now the main eccentrics start their quarrel on the
> sheaves:
> Her time, her own appointed time, the rocking link-head
> bides,

> Till – hear that note? – the rod's return wings glimmerin'
> through the guides.

His curiosity for technical terms and process was insatiable. Seamen and engineers, architects and gold-miners, scientists and surgeons – no-one was safe from his relentless questioning. On his many journeys to and from South Africa, we are told that the officers of the Union Castle Line dreaded him, and prayed not to find themselves on the same ship, since they were invariably buttonholed and then cross-examined about their work for hours at a time until they felt like squeezed lemons. (Though even this did not stop Kipling, on one occasion, from reporting the whole lot of them on arrival in England for flirting with the passengers.)

By now, too, Kipling had found his length. After *Kim* he wrote no more novels; apart from the occasional ventures into politics like *The Years Between*, his history of the Irish Guards in the Great War and his deeply undistinguished experiment in autobiography that I have already mentioned, he stuck to the short poem, and the short story. I have said comparatively little so far about Kipling's short stories. Many, I may as well confess, I find unreadable. I cannot bear the sham dialect of *Soldiers Three* and a good many others like it; for that reason alone the beauty of *Love-o'-Women*, which no less a critic than Maurice Baring considered among his best, is lost on me. Nor can I willingly endure the slapstick of *My Sunday at Home* or *Brugglesmith,* or the cruel practical jokery of such tales as *The Village that Voted the Earth was Flat.* There can be little doubt, on the other hand, that in his best short stories Kipling surpasses any other writer in English – and does so at every stage in his career. Some masterpieces, *The Man who would be King* for example, date from as early as the 1880s; others, like *They* – one of the most beautiful of all his stories – from the early 1900s. The dreadful but unforgettable *Mary Postgate* appeared in 1917; the most poignant, *The Gardener,* as late as 1926. This is the story of a woman wandering through a military cemetery in France, looking for the grave of the illegitimate son she has never acknowledged.

> A man knelt behind a line of headstones – evidently a gardener, for he was firming a young plant in the soft earth. She went towards him, her paper in her hand. He rose at her approach and without prelude or salutation asked: 'Who are you looking for?'
>
> 'Lieutenant Michael Turrell – my nephew,' said Helen slowly and word for word, as she had many thousands of times in her life.
>
> The man lifted his eyes and looked at her with infinite compassion before he turned from the fresh-sown grass toward the naked black crosses.
>
> 'Come with me,' he said, 'and I will show you where your son lies.'
>
> When Helen left the cemetery she turned for a last look. In the distance she saw the man bending over his young plants; and she went away, supposing him to be the gardener.

In the 1920s that final reference to St John's Gospel would, I suspect, have been a good deal better known than it is today.

Does Rudyard Kipling deserve his reputation? Before trying to answer that question, we have to establish just what that reputation is. Few writers in all literature are more loved or more loathed: as C. S. Lewis wrote, 'hardly any reader likes him a little'. On his second return from India, as we have seen, he had taken London by storm, and ten years later his fame had spread all over the world. In Russia, I am told, he is still the best-known of all English writers, Shakespeare not excepted. In his own country, however, though he remained a celebrity to the end of his life and his books continued to sell in huge numbers, his reputation began to decline soon after the Boer

War; and it comes as something of a surprise to read that already in Edwardian days the literary world had ceased to take him seriously, seeing him as facile, superficial and hopelessly outdated. In particular his award of the Nobel Prize for Literature in 1907 attracted a howl of protest, and has been roundly condemned on countless occasions since.

Yet he remains a giant: frequently vulgar and tasteless (as is the way of giants) and occasionally downright nauseating, but a giant none the less. What is more, he was his own giant. His subject matter, his viewpoint, his opinions, his style both in verse and prose – all were his and his alone. Few writers have owed less to their predecessors, just as few have given more to the language. His values may not be our values – though they are a good deal more likely to be now than they were thirty or forty years ago – but however firmly we may reject them we cannot deny the brilliance with which they are expressed and which has, in a very real sense, given them immortality.

Let me end, as I began, with a poem – which seems to me to summarise his philosophy better than most:

When Earth's last picture is painted and the tubes are
                                    twisted and dried,
When the oldest colours have faded, and the youngest critic
                                    has died,
We shall rest, and, faith, we shall need it – lie down for an
                                    aeon or two,
Till the Master of All Good Workmen shall put us to work
                                    anew.

And those that were good shall be happy: they shall sit in a
                                    golden chair;
They shall splash at a ten-league canvas with brushes of
                                    comets' hair.

They shall find real saints to draw from – Magdalene, Peter
and Paul;
They shall work for an age at a sitting and never be tired at
all!

And only The Master shall praise us, and only The Master
shall blame;
And no one shall work for money, and no one shall work for
fame,
But each for the joy of the working, and each, in his separate
star,
Shall draw the Thing as he sees It for the God of Things as
They are!

Perhaps he did deserve the Nobel Prize after all.

HAROLD NICOLSON

1886–1968

KENNETH ROSE

HAROLD NICOLSON

THE LONDON LIBRARY, in common with other great institutions such as 10 Downing Street, Scotland Yard and the MCC,
cherishes its private pantheon: the collected portraits of those
who have guided its fortunes over the years. All who ascend the
main staircase of No. 14 St James's Square are greeted by just
such a gallery of likenesses, many of which belong to history.
There is the mournful countenance of Arthur Balfour, for
instance, pondering the folly of having exchanged the role of
philosopher for that of a mere Prime Minister; there are the
severe features of T. S. Eliot to discourage all but the serious-
minded from publishing and poetry alike.

But who, the younger reader may wonder, who is the old
gentleman hanging between them, with alert yet kindly eyes and
a neat military moustache? A brigadier, perhaps, who has retired
to Bournemouth to collect stamps? No, it is Sir Harold Nicolson
who, as it happened, detested Bournemouth, brigadiers and
stamp collecting with equal fervour. He was a member of the
committee of the London Library for twenty years and our
Chairman for another six. He was held in high affection by all
who knew him and he lives on in many hearts. Books were the
stuff of his life; what he drew from the library shelves in pleasure
and knowledge, he returned in devoted service. He was a generous benefactor. When the Westminster City Council threatened
the existence of our library by imposing a heavy and unexpected
burden of rates, he sent for sale the most valuable book in his

library, Moore's *Life of Byron*, annotated by John Cam Hobhouse. That and many other contributions saved the day.

Although Harold was assiduous in his duties, he did not always display those brisk and businesslike qualities that are to be found in the chairman of a merchant bank or of a chain of supermarkets. 'On one occasion,' John Wells writes in his evocative new history of the library, 'Nicolson suggested as a possible candidate for the committee, though not in particularly flattering terms, a man who was sitting beside him at the table'. He used to say that the committee of the London Library was the most intelligent he had ever known: quite gratifying when one remembers that he had hovered in attendance on Lloyd George and Balfour at the Paris Peace Conference of 1919 and carried Lord Curzon's green baize footrest at Lausanne four years later; that he had subsequently adorned the committees of the National Trust, the National Portrait Gallery, the Classical Association and other bodies of equal respectability.

Harold Nicolson was almost literally born into diplomacy. At the time of his birth in 1886 his father was Secretary of Legation in Tehran. Arthur Nicolson, later created Lord Carnock, came of an old Scottish family and was heir to a seventeenth-century baronetcy. This dignity, however, was unsupported by either landed estates or a private income. So he joined the Diplomatic Service, rising to its summit as ambassador in St Petersburg and retiring in 1916 as Permanent Under-Secretary of the Foreign Office. He led the sober, industrious life of a professional public servant and epitomised all that is most admired and respected in his calling. In contemplating a diplomatic career for his third son, he could rely not only on his own example but also upon the considerable influence of his brother-in-law Lord Dufferin: Governor-General of Canada, Viceroy of India, ambassador in St Petersburg and in Paris.

Harold went to school at Wellington, where he was so miserable and bored that it was twenty-seven years before he could bring himself to return. That intrepid Field-Marshal Sir Gerald Templer, he once told me, was another unhappy Wellingtonian who delayed revisiting the school until well into middle age. He was liberated by Balliol. 'I am always carried away by the mention of Oxford,' he wrote in later years, 'even on a pot of marmalade'. The aesthete who in his life of King George V shuddered at York Cottage, Sandringham, 'a glum little villa . . . indistinguishable from any Surbiton or Upper Norwood home,' found nothing to criticise in the penitential stones of his old college. He did, however, confess to a lifetime of 'shame and remorse' at taking only a Third in Greats. He need not have worried: it was a degree respectable enough to share with those two eminent Foreign Secretaries, Sir Edward Grey and Lord Home of the Hirsel. In any case, his lapse was surely forgiven when in 1953 Balliol elected him to what he called the greatest honour of his life: an honorary Fellowship of the College.

In 1909 Harold took second place in the stiff examination for the Diplomatic Service, beaten only by the future Minister of Education, Lord Eustace Percy. He was well-equipped for his chosen career: clever, alert, industrious, precise, loyal and sociable. He had, moreover, spent his early years in Persia, Hungary, Bulgaria and Morocco. And although in time he came to detest almost all foreigners except the French and the Greeks, that was not in itself an impediment to advancement in the Diplomatic Service. He served first as a junior clerk in the Foreign Office, then at our embassies in Madrid and Constantinople. He liked to recall one of his few blunders. When instructed by our ambassador in Constantinople to congratulate one consul on being awarded a CMG and to rebuke another for lateness in submitting a report, he contrived that each should receive the telegram meant for the other.

He returned to the Foreign Office in 1914, just in time to play his first role on the world stage. It was a walk-on part: literally so. In the last hours of peace, the Foreign Office had sent the

German ambassador in London a wrongly worded declaration of war; at least they got the country right. It fell to Nicolson, as the most junior member of the staff available, to walk across to the German embassy late at night, wake up the ambassador, retrieve the defective document and substitute a correct version. That embarrassing duty was a prelude to more important tasks. Already recognised as a man of unusual ability, he was forbidden to enlist in the Army. Within two years he was drafting memoranda on foreign policy for the War Cabinet. In 1919 he became an indispensable member of the British delegation to the Peace Conference, a trusted adviser to both Lloyd George and Balfour, a draughtsman of the Treaty of Versailles, that changed the course of history. But then, as Winston Churchill used to say, something is always changing the course of history.

It was at the Paris conference that he began keeping the diary on which much of his literary fame may ultimately rest: a legacy more enduring perhaps than the Treaty of Versailles itself. Already he was a master of the illuminating anecdote. After the official opening of the conference, he records, Balfour walked down the steps with Clemenceau, Balfour wearing a top hat, Clemenceau a bowler. 'I was told,' Balfour said plaintively, 'that it was obligatory to wear a top hat.' Clemenceau replied: 'So was I'. Later Nicolson asked Balfour what he thought of the supposed rudeness of an ailing German delegate in not standing up when replying to Clemenceau. 'Didn't he stand up?' Balfour said. 'I failed to notice. I make it a rule never to stare at people when they are in obvious distress.'

Then there was the evening that Nicolson dined at the Ritz with the Polish nobleman Joseph Potocki and praised the speech of President Paderewski, the Vaclav Havel of his time, to the Supreme Council. 'Yes,' Potocki replied, 'a remarkable man, a very remarkable man. Do you realise that he was born in one of my own villages? And yet when I speak to him I have absolutely the impression of conversing with an equal.'

Edward Gibbon wrote that 'the Captain of the Hampshire Grenadiers has not been useless to the historian of the Roman Empire'. Nicolson similarly put his practical experience of diplomacy to good use in a succession of volumes of diplomatic history alluringly disguised as biography. He wrote the life of his father Lord Carnock and of his uncle Lord Dufferin; a sparkling personal account of the Peace Conference; an inimitable portrait of Lord Curzon's years at the Foreign Office.

There was even a novel entitled *Public Faces*, published in 1932, in which he foretold with extraordinary prescience the invention of the atom bomb and its influence on diplomacy – a device 'no bigger than an inkstand that could by the discharge of its electrons destroy New York.'

All his books with a diplomatic theme were permeated by an insight denied to the layman. 'Nobody,' he wrote in his account of the Congress of Vienna, 'who has not actually watched statesmen dealing with each other can have any real idea of the immense part played in human affairs by such unavowable and often unrecognisable causes as lassitude, affability, personal affection or dislike, misunderstanding, deafness or incomplete command of a foreign language, vanity, social engagements, interruptions and momentary states of health.' With such a warning, Harold Nicolson has put all historians in his debt.

Throughout the First World War, Harold toiled away in the Foreign Office, burdened by a sense of deep insecurity in his private life. In 1913 he had married Vita Sackville-West, only daughter of the Third Lord Sackville. It was an unusual marriage, for both partners preferred to find sexual satisfaction with members of their own sex. That did not preclude Vita from bearing Harold two sons. Ben achieved distinction as an art historian, his brother Nigel as publisher and writer of several elegant books that include *Portrait of a Marriage*. It is the privilege of a son to unveil the emotional lives of his parents, and I shall scarcely trespass on his ground.

But what cannot be omitted from any portrait of Harold Nicolson is that whereas he was discreet in his sexual life, his wife was not. He was what the French call *légèrement pédéraste*. No member of the Diplomatic Service seventy years ago could have afforded to be too demonstrative in his homosexual pursuits without risking professional suicide. Behind that military moustache and bustling presence, Harold conducted himself with decorum. His affairs were discreet and largely with his own class, including more than one member of the Diplomatic Service who rose to high rank. He was not tempted to take young men on educative visits to the opera – if only because he had no ear for music. Vita, by contrast, was torrid in her entanglements, eloping more than once with her chosen partner. These distracting scandals caused Harold embarrassment and distress throughout the war and in the immediate years that followed. As James Lees-Milne has written in his affectionate yet scrupulously just biography: 'His attitude was quite unlike that of any known husband in love with a wife who was having a passionate affair with somebody else, let alone a woman.' There were, it must be said, discreditable incidents on his part. Yet on balance he emerges with a kindness, tolerance and tact towards his wife that were not reciprocated.

Harold and Vita nevertheless loved each other profoundly for almost half a century. It was a love lacking only in the physical, an affair of the heart and of the mind. If she went out for five minutes to post a letter, he would deliquesce into an agony of apprehension until her safe return. When separated, he wrote to her daily, sometimes almost hourly. On the day he left for Persia in 1925 to take up his appointment in the British Legation at Tehran, he sent her four letters: in the train to Dover, on the Channel steamer, in Calais and on the train to Paris. But he did find some comfort on that bleakest of days. 'A perfect dream of a steward has just come for my luggage,' he told his wife in letter number two.

Ultimately she drove him out of diplomacy. Promoted and decorated with the CMG at thirty-three for his work in Paris, he went on to become assistant to the first Secretary-general of the League of Nations, then private secretary to the formidable Lord Curzon. There followed postings to Persia and Berlin. He was in sight of being given his own embassy. But Vita refused to accompany her husband abroad, though she did visit him briefly. She hated the constrictions of diplomatic life; the need to be polite to people she considered inferior both socially and intellectually; all State and ceremonial occasions that required her to wear fine clothes and jewels. In Persia, however, she did agree to accompany her husband to the Coronation of the Shah and to wear the family emeralds from Knole. On returning to their house in Tehran she found that her large emerald pendant was missing. So they drove back to the palace. There they discovered the Prime Minister on his knees, emerald in hand, trying to fit it into the Peacock Throne from which he supposed it had been dislodged. 'Your Highness,' Harold shouted, 'that emerald belongs to my wife.'

Vita's refusal to share Harold's career abroad was not the only spur to his disenchantment with diplomacy. For the past decade he had devoted his leisure to writing and now wished to be rid of the constraints imposed upon any public servants with literary tastes. Perhaps unconsciously, he had felt obliged to sanitize the studies of poets and poetry which he published throughout the 1920s: Verlaine without a homosexual theme, Swinburne without flagellation, Byron without incest. How much more he might achieve when freed from the genteel suspicions of Downing Street and Whitehall.

In 1927 came the best-known of all his books: that lively squib of fictional autobiography and autobiographical fiction called *Some People*. As a matter of fact, I am not at all sure that *Some People* is the correct pronunciation. The accent should surely be on the second word. One does not say, 'I am going to see some people', but 'I am going to see some *people*'. The book has long delighted the reading public. The author, who had written it largely to amuse himself and who doubted whether it was worth publishing, took little pleasure in its popular success. He observed unamiably that it was the one book of his which would be remembered by old ladies, the proletariat and the Earl of Athlone.

The effect of *Some People* on his fellow diplomats was distinctly lowering. As Harold admitted: 'My bad habit of ridiculing everybody from myself upwards may often land me in appearances of disloyalty.' His father, Lord Carnock, was deeply pained. Sir Percy Loraine, under whom Harold had served in Persia, discerned something of himself in the fictional Lord Bognor and declared it to be 'a cad's book'. Later that year, Harold asked if he could be posted to Rome. But the ambassador, fearing that his new counsellor might one day mock him in print, refused. So he was posted to Berlin, where the resident ambassador expressed similar alarm. Clive Bell, while praising the intelligence and wit of *Some People*, doubted whether it was the book of a future ambassador. He was right. In 1929 Harold resigned.

Virginia Woolf, who had been one of Vita's lovers, wrote to her sister: 'Apparently diplomatic society is so boring that he can't face ever becoming an ambassador. Really I do think it's a feather in Bloomsbury's cap, a goose feather if you like.' But Harold had no intention of being drawn into the Bloomsbury orbit. He was repelled by their sneers and sniggers, by their narrowness of sympathy and want of compassion, by their assumption of an ill-founded moral and intellectual superiority. He had spent twenty years pursuing a foreign policy that he thought honourable and, with occasional lapses, benevolent. He resented their drip of denigration. For Lytton Strachey he harboured a rare, savage dislike. 'I shall *not* become a flabby old sod like Lytton,' he wrote, 'I won't, I won't, I won't.' And on reading the Lytton-Virginia letters in 1956 he was appalled 'by their silliness, dirtiness and cattishness'.

In resigning from the Diplomatic Service, Harold had regained both his wife and his literary freedom. There was a third reason. He needed more money. He had two boys to be educated at Eton and the upkeep of three establishments: rooms in King's Bench Walk; Long Barn, his enlarged cottage near Sevenoaks; and the recently acquired Sissinghurst, where Harold designed and Vita planted one of the loveliest gardens in England. So he allowed himself to be lured to the *Evening Standard* at a comfortable salary as a contributor to its 'Londoner's Diary'. He stood it for no more than eighteen months. Others have adjusted themselves to writing both literary biography and a newspaper column without suffering more than an occasional nervous breakdown. Harold could never come to terms with popular journalism either professionally or socially; nor was he robust enough to shrug off the pressures of his proprietor, that inspired buccaneer Lord Beaverbrook.

His next move was even more unfortunate. Attracted by the romance of politics, he attached himself to the court of another stormy petrel, Sir Oswald Mosley, unsuccessfully fighting a parliamentary seat on behalf of the New Party and editing its newspaper, *Action*. In ten weeks its circulation fell from 160,000 to 16,000. Harold's heart was not really in it, though he came near to halting the Blackshirt Movement in its stride by suggesting a uniform of *grey* shirts and trousers for Mosley's men. When the New Party began to show signs of thuggery and anti-semitism, Harold took his leave. By temperament an Asquithian Liberal, he had made a disastrous debut on the political stage. In 1935, however, he found an uneasy foothold in the National Labour party; the rump of those few who in 1931 had crossed the floor of the House with Ramsay MacDonald on the formation of a predominantly Conservative 'National' Government. It was a party with an amorphous programme and no future: but it did provide Harold with a seat in the Commons from 1935 to 1945. He concentrated upon foreign affairs and his maiden speech on Abyssinia and the League of Nations was much admired. He also showed consistent courage in supporting Churchill's call for rearmament against the dictators. At the time of the Munich agreement, he not only refused to support Chamberlain's government, but remained seated when a briefly triumphant Prime Minister entered the House. 'Stand up, you brute,' a Conservative Member snarled at him.

On the formation of Churchill's Coalition Government in 1940, Harold was rewarded with ministerial office. As Parliamentary Secretary to the Ministry of Information under Duff Cooper he put his Liberal instincts to good use by appealing for the humane treatment of German refugees even in a climate of fear and xenophobia; and by trying to mitigate the harshness of regulations that could send a mindless chatterbox to jail for even the mildest of defeatist remarks. He himself was as intrepid as any throughout the Blitz. Nor had the Prime Minister a more loyal supporter. 'My God,' he wrote, 'my love and admiration of Winston surge round me like a tide'. It was not entirely reciprocated. After little more than a year in office, Harold had to surrender his post to a Labour member in order to maintain the political balance of the Coalition Government; but there is more than a suspicion that the Prime Minister had not thought Harold formidable enough as a wartime minister. He was consoled with a seat on the governing body of the BBC and at the end of the war a medal engraved: 'Salute the Great Coalition'.

It was characteristic of Harold's patriotism that on being sacked from the Government he voluntarily went to work as a part-time munitions worker – he, the clumsiest man with his hands who ever lived. When in Persia he had managed to break a column at Persepolis that had withstood the ravages of 2,000 years; and he nearly put an end to a long friendship with the Duke of Wellington by damaging first a valuable snuff-box, then a Rolls-Royce. The inspectors at the munitions factory used to place his finished parts in a box labelled NG. He assumed it stood for 'No Good' – and he took the hint.

If few of Harold's shell-cases or tank parts helped us towards victory, he did perform a more oblique service to the Allied cause. From the months he spent in Paris polishing his command of the language for the Foreign Office exam, he had come to love all things French. It found expression in his championship of General de Gaulle and the Free French Forces both on the BBC and in the Press. Churchill looked on the General as an irritant; Nicolson accepted that anyone cast in the role of his country's saviour in exile would have displayed the same intransigence, even arrogance, in preserving the honour and independence of France. In March 1945 Harold was able to visit Paris once more. As he came down the gangway of the Channel steamer at Calais, he bent down to touch the soil of France. The porter carrying his baggage turned round and asked:

'*Monsieur a laissé tomber quelque chose?*'

'*Non,*' Harold replied, '*j'ai retrouvé quelque chose.*'

Labour's landslide victory in the general election of 1945 cost Harold the seat in the House of Commons he had held for ten years. He missed it. He missed the vantage point from which to observe the unfolding of history and those quirks of human character which leave their mark on great events. He missed a platform from which to make known his views on foreign policy. He missed the camaraderie and the gossip. Nor was there much chance of his being adopted for another constituency. He was repelled as much by the rigidity of socialist doctrine as by the heartlessness of Tory behaviour. 'Do you not think that the Conservatives trample on the faces of the poor?' he was asked at a political meeting. 'No,' he replied judiciously, 'but I am afraid that they do not always look where they put their feet.'

He would have been ideally suited to a university seat, but the new Labour Government had let it be known that they proposed to abolish them – as indeed they did. There were no cross benches in the Commons. There were, however in the House of Lords. So he discreetly asked whether he might not be made a peer: and what an adornment he would have been to the Upper House. Indeed, there is evidence that such an offer had been made informally to him by Anthony Eden in 1944, but that Harold had preferred to take his chance on continuing in the House of Commons. In asking the new Labour Government for a peerage, he attached what he should have known would be unacceptable conditions: that he would be expected neither to take the Labour whip nor speak against Winston Churchill. So he waited in vain. Eventually, pocketing his pride, he applied for membership of the Labour Party, hoping that this would now open the door to that gilded chamber, those crimson benches; at least he could with a clear conscience support Labour's foreign policy in the hands of Ernest Bevin.

Harold's change of political allegiance was received with astonishment. 'I suppose,' his brother observed, 'he will now have to resign from all his clubs.' That was nonsense. But he did have to join the sort of club he had never before encountered, where one ate liver and onions and sang 'The Red Flag'. That *via dolorosa*, however, led him not to the House of Lords, but to the drab suburbs of Croydon, where he was required to fight a Commons by-election on behalf of his new party.

He loathed every moment of it, not least the false bonhomie required of him; nor was he ever at ease with working class electors. Vita refused to share his misery by accompanying him on his canvassing tours, just as she had abandoned him to his lonely missions in Tehran and Berlin. So night after night he sat alone in his dismal hotel bedroom making Ovaltine over a gas ring. He lost the election. But it was not the increase in the Tory majority from 600 to 12,000 which ultimately cost him that elusive peerage. Rather was it a mocking, self-deprecating article

he wrote about the election for the *Spectator*. The Labour Party
constituency workers had believed in their outlandishly patrician
candidate, had strained every nerve to help him. He had
responded by making them characters in a dreary, painful,
embarrassing and oh-so-common charade. As Nigel Nicolson
wrote of this final phase of his father's political career, it was
damned 'by 1500 words which he typed, more out of amusement
than pique, on an empty Sunday afternoon'.

What made the loss harder to bear was the discovery some
months later of just how near he had come to receiving a peerage
before the distressing episode of the Croydon by-election. Lord
Longford – whom I am delighted to see here tonight with Lady
Longford, fresh from the celebration last night of their Golden
Wedding – Lord Longford later told Harold that his name had
been included in an early draft of the Honours list to be published in January 1948. The Prime Minister, Mr Attlee, then
noticed that Vita's name was already in the same list, to be
made a Companion of Honour in recognition of one of the most
admired poets of the day. So he decided that Harold's peerage
must await the next Honours list six months later. But by then
the Croydon by-election had intervened, robbing Harold of the
Labour Party goodwill on which his honour depended. It was
just such a quirk of history that in other circumstances he
delighted to expound.

There is one more footnote to be added. When Harold's
diaries were published more than twenty years later, critics
fastened on to this passage: 'I am amused to find in myself a fat
grub of snobbishness. I have always hated the name Nicolson
as being a common plebian name. . . . If I were made a real peer
I could change it to Cranfield'. This and similar sentiments
exposed his memory to some ridicule. The would-be Lord Cranfield was not without traces of snobbishness: but he was also
addicted to making jokes against himself, a dangerous practice
in an age of grudge and envy. He wanted to be a peer, not

because he craved the obsequious greeting of a maître d'hotel but because he wanted a seat at Westminster.

He nevertheless settled down to happy sunset years, broken only by Vita's death in 1962. A Trollope-like regime governed his life as a writer. From Friday to Tuesday each week he would be at Sissinghurst, sometimes in the garden, more often tapping away at his typewriter. The rest of the week he spent in his rooms in Albany, a welcoming host and lovable friend. He was much in demand as a lecturer and broadcaster, a coveted guest at many tables and a pillar of the Beefsteak Club. In later years Vita would join him for an annual ocean cruise. He rarely cared to go ashore during those voyages: sometimes because he disapproved of the country's political regime, more because he disliked almost all foreigners. I often wondered where the sherry he gave us had come from, for he thought Franco's Spain and South African apartheid equally detestable.

Harold was an enviably industrious and fluent writer, able to turn out 5,000 flawless words a day with ease. During one weekend in 1946, for instance, he produced his weekly 'Marginal Comment' for the *Spectator*; one article for the BBC Year Book, another for *Contact* magazine, a third for *Le Figaro*; two book reviews and two talks for the BBC. He read prodigiously, too. And here let me pass on a tip he gave me many years ago which I have found immensely valuable: always make your own index in any book you read.

In addition to his more formal works, Harold also produced a substantial volume a year that was not to be published until near the end of his life: his diaries. First there was his sparkling account of the Paris Peace Conference of 1919, then a pause until in 1930 he began to sit down daily at his typewriter to record the impressions of the previous day. And how grateful we are not only to the author but also to his son Nigel for his exemplary editing of them. Harold could be far sharper in his comments on friends and acquaintances than the reader of the edited version may suppose. Yet Nigel has ensured that all, or almost all, shall be sweetness and light. The dead he left to look after themselves, so that we are permitted to read Harold's verdict on a lady at whose house he often lunched: 'She is nothing more than a fat slug filled with venom'. But Nigel has always tried to spare pain to the living in editing his father's diaries. I remember lunching with him one day at Sissinghurst during the last years of his father's life, when he told me how one public figure was angrily disputing the remarks attributed to him by Harold in his diary and was threatening legal action. 'But have you not heard?' I told Nigel. 'The man has died.' 'Oh,' said Nigel, 'what a relief. You *have* earned your lunch.'

And so, in spite of a little discreet censorship, we are left with three volumes of the utmost historical importance, a rich and luminous tapestry of our time. An accomplished impresario, he draws his cast of thousands from the overlapping worlds of politics, literature, diplomacy and the arts, spiced by the merely royal or social. Not even P. G. Wodehouse can match him in the striking of the memorable phrase. After sitting between Margot Asquith and Violet Bonham Carter, he tells us it is like being massaged by two Kurds; and he describes Winston Churchill as resembling 'the Chinese god of plenty suffering from acute indigestion'.

Diarists are not always upon oath. They are artists. They select, omit, arrange, sometimes even nudge events into a harmonious or dramatic pattern. Let me give an example. Here is a charming description which Harold wrote for the *Spectator* of an evening at Magdalene College, Cambridge, with Sir Stephen Gaselee, the learned librarian of the Foreign Office, and A. E. Housman:

The food was well cooked and chosen; the several vintages were superb. I sat there late into the night listening to the two scholars discussing prosody. Housman rapped out the metres with a dry hand upon the mahogany; the glasses tinkled as he did so; Gaselee, with a deft mixture of deference and contradiction, soothed that prickly soul. On and on they went talking about dochmiacs and choriambs. The bells of Cambridge echoed solemnly around us.

Charming, is it not? Three high-minded scholars discussing prosody late into the night. That was written thirteen years after the event. Here is what Harold wrote at the time:

We have 1789 Madeira and Haut Brion and tripe and oysters and grouse-pie and mushrooms. The firelight flits on the silver of the smaller combination room and there are red shades, highly inflammable, to each candle. Housman is dry, soft, shy, prickly . . . greedy, and a touch of a toper. 'What is this, my dear Gaselee?' 'This is Estrella 1789.' 'A perfect wine.' Yet not eighteenth-century and still less 1890. A *bon bourgeois* who has seen more sensitive days. He does not talk much except about food. And at 10.30 he rises to take his leave.

So there we are: no talk of prosody, of dochmiacs and choriambs late into the night. Just three well-nourished gentlemen gossiping about food and wine, followed by an early bed. Even in the rarified air of Magdalene College, Cambridge, one pays one's money and one takes one's choice.

In 1952 Harold published what many consider to be his *magnum opus*, the official life of King George V. It is a majestic and illuminating work that blends the human with the historic. It also triumphs over certain restraints. When he began his research in 1948, the King had been dead only twelve years, and his widow and children were still very much alive. Harold was told by King George VI's private secretary that what he must write was a book about a national institution from which all discreditable episodes, if any, should be omitted.

Following in his footsteps a generation later, and released from official inhibitions of deference and taste, I marvelled at how deftly he had satisfied both the demands of the courtier and the conscience of the historian. Here and there I discovered that Harold had glossed over or sanitized some contentious act of the King's: his abrupt change of mind in 1917, for instance, that denied asylum to his deposed Russian cousin, the Tsar, and ultimately cost that monarch his life. Or the unconstitutional partisanship, even enmity, with which the King took the side of Admiral Beresford in the feud with Admiral Fisher that split the Royal Navy for a whole generation. But how much remains that for all time places the King in his true historical perspective; and with what grace and clarity he unfolds his tale.

King George V brought his official biographer universal acclaim, near-bankruptcy and a knighthood. The first gave him modest pleasure: the last two did not. Although the book's royalties swelled his always exiguous bank balance, he forgot that he would have to pay tax on his new-found affluence, and the Inland Revenue pursued him for the rest of his life. As for the Knighthood of the Royal Victorian Order which the Queen offered to her grandfather's biographer, he thought it rather a middle-class reward, the sort of thing a provincial mayor might relish. 'I would rather have a dozen bottles of champagne or a travelling clock,' he wrote. In the end, like Maria Theresa at the Partition of Poland, he wept but he took.

In this patrician scorn for the lesser honours we can discern the hand of Vita, who taught her husband the Sackville word *bedint*, from the German *bedienen*, to serve. It can be used either as a noun or an adjective, and means genteel, vulgar or common. Vita, for instance, did not like diplomacy, because it meant 'taking trouble about a lot of bedints'. It was bedint to have a knighthood and even more bedint to have an MBE, as did her son Nigel. It was bedint to shop at the Army and Navy Stores or to live in Cadogan Gardens, as did Lord and Lady Carnock. It was bedint for a husband and wife to share a dressing table in life or to have their ashes mingled in death. It was bedint to be American and even more unfortunate to be Jewish or Black. Really, what problems Vita and Harold caused themselves.

Yet through that miasma of prejudice shone a glow of pure gold. Harold might affect to dislike Jews and Blacks, but he disliked injustice more; and refugees from oppression could always depend upon his help, whatever their origins. Nor did he impose any test of manners, morals or sobriety on those who sought his charity. 'It will be a great economy for us,' his secretary Miss Niggeman used to say, 'when all your friends are in prison.'

Well, here is one of them still at liberty, who never ceases to recall Harold's kindness over the years. There was the occasion when the owner of some historic letters I wished to consult for a book was reluctant to part with them because they might contain indiscretions. I mentioned this to Harold, who at once suggested to the owner that he himself would go through them, extracting all that could be safely made known. He handed me the notes he had made a few days later : they ran to seven quarto sheets closely typed in his own hand.

How funny he was, too, in his teasing. I treasure the postcard he wrote after dining with me one night: 'You are a wonderful cook, and if all else failed could make a large income at the Midland Hotel, Manchester.'

The death of Vita in 1962 was a blow from which he never recovered. For a year or two he continued to divide the week between Sissinghurst and Albany, but increasingly enveloped in melancholy and beset by the physical ailments of old age. Then he retired to the country, which he never again left. He lost the will to write, then to read, even to talk: a solitary mourner, as

Rosebery said of Lord Randolph Churchill, 'a solitary mourner at his own protracted funeral'.

But it was not quite the end. He found comfort in the presence of Nigel and his family – and I hope he came to regret the flamboyant aesthetic judgement he had made public during the war: that he would rather his son were killed at Cassino than that the monastery should be destroyed.

On his eightieth birthday I was invited to join the family at Sissinghurst for a celebration, and by some miracle the clouds rolled away for an hour or two. Harold sat down to dinner in high spirits, ate foie gras and pheasant, drank sherry and champagne, opened his birthday presents, criticised with refreshing bluntness a drawing of Vita by Sir William Rothenstein that was among them. 'Vita was a beautiful woman,' he said, 'and that is an ugly one.'

After dinner he smoked some Persian cigarettes I had brought from his birthplace, Tehran, and he was persuaded to chant a verse or two of Omar Khayyam in Farsee. He strove to recollect happy moments from the past, told us how few regrets he had of life and went off to bed.

I think affectionately of Harold Nicolson every time I pass the photograph on the stairs of the London Library, and I hope you will do so too.

ROSE MACAULAY

1881–1958

A.N. WILSON

ROSE MACAULAY

AT THE PARTY held to celebrate the 150th anniversary of the London Library, a voice was heard in that crowded scene in St James's Square: 'Is Rose Macaulay here?' Since it is thirty-three years since Rose Macaulay died, the inquirer must have been either singularly out of touch, or singularly In Touch – the casual social inquiry takes on the tone of a medium, making inquiry of the spirits at a seance. The question was written up in the newspaper; but we do not know how it was answered. We do not know if Rose Macaulay chose to abandon the Elysian Fields for an evening party. Certainly in life – and that was the point of the inquiry in St James's Square – she was an insatiable party-goer – usually the first to arrive, and the last to leave – and could be found, tall, willowy, upright, to the end of her days, standing in the middle of crowded rooms talking – of books, politics, religion, the ancient world, and of the exotic places in Eastern Turkey and the Mediterranean which she loved so well. On a cruise in those parts during the last years of her life, she agreed to take part in a Brains Trust to entertain her fellow-passengers. One of the questions was a simple one, to the effect – 'What other life would you have wished for?' The other panellists bumbled and mumbled, and said that they wanted peace in the world, or happy family life. When it came to Rose's turn, she raised her thin old arm and said in that voice redolent of all her learned relations and ancestors, 'A LIFE – WITH ABSOLUTE POWER!'

129

John Wells, the historian of the London Library, describes the morning in St James's Square after the library was hit by a bomb. Mr Cox arrived from Wimbledon as usual and found that the roof was off and the top storey burnt out. One member of the library is alleged to have emerged from the burnt out stacks on the top floor and said to Mr Cox – 'We've lost our Religion'. Higher up than the lost religion, staff and members were struggling to save as many books as possible from the wreckage. A tangle of girders stretched out like tormented fingers to the open sky. Everything was covered with grey dust, and shelves of books, apparently suspended on air, dangled precariously in the sky, in imminent danger of being wrecked by rain, having been spared by fire. Joan Bailey and James Lees-Milne were there, but, we are told, Rose Macaulay was the bravest, telling them to hang on to her legs as she leant out into space.

There is something so haunting about this, recalling the monks of whom we read at school – whether figures of legend or not it makes no odds – who fled from the ruins of Constantinople with their books and manuscripts under their arms. She herself lost everything in the Blitz, when her flat was hit by the Luftwaffe, and her work in progress, her library and all her possessions were destroyed. 'I now have nothing,' she wrote. 'I came up from Liss last night to find Luxborough House is no more – bombed and burnt out of existence, and nothing saved. I am bookless, homeless, *sans* everything but my eyes to weep with . . . I've lost my Pliny, Topsell, Sylvester, everything. Isn't that desolating.' To another friend, she wrote that 'my lost books leave a gaping wound in my heart and mind'.

Of course, after the desolations of the war, Rose Macaulay rather famously and heroically rebuilt her life, and found once more that it was possible to replace lost treasures, such as her complete *Oxford Dictionary*, just as it was possible to recover religious faith. But something had gone. Hers is an essentially elegiac voice, though not always deliberately so. The Whiggish, high-minded, well-read – and though she was herself at the Oxford High School and Somerville, I should say rather Cambridgey – people from whom she came – the generation of dons, and learned persons and liberals with large and small ls from whom she sprang had indeed, once upon a time, exercised, if not ABSOLUTE POWER, then something very like it in the days when Thomas Babington Macaulay occupied his rooms in Albany and wrote histories to show that everything was getting better and better – higher standards of political decency, saner values, greater social justice, thanks to the Whigs, who from 1642, 1689, 1714, 1832 had been achieving ABSOLUTE POWER and spreading sweetness and light as they did so – and that time was over. England, Europe, the Western World was no longer run by decent, educated persons such as her own family were. Other forces and figures, about whom she had been consistently shrill and snobbish in her earlier books, had taken it over. In her last decade, she was indeed scrambling bravely in the ruins, reaching towards the blank sky with scrawny hand to see whether Pliny or Topsell or Sylvester could be rescued from extinction. She knew it was a losing battle in a world where the numbers of those who had so much as heard of Pliny were diminishing all the time. The debacle had happened, and like the crowds that flowed over London bridge, men were scurrying from the burnt-out stacks and saying, 'We've lost our religion'.

I suppose that it is because she belonged so firmly, so intransigently to her own class and family that Rose Macaulay has not survived. Even the stories which we still, a little condescendingly, tell about her suggest that she was an eccentric, a freak, a donnish relic of a world which was obsolete, if not a wilderness, even before she left it. I am thinking of such stories of Rose serving on a committee set up to advise the BBC on pronunciation. How should announcers on the wireless pronounce the word SAUSAGE? Various minds, including that of George Bernard Shaw, were expected to advise Lord Reith on this question, but the discussion was interrupted by Rose. It was not, she said, a matter of debate. The word was pronounced SORSIJ.

I wince a little now to re-read some of her earlier books where she is so firmly on the war-path against Potterism as she called it. Mr Percy Potter, the self-made man who has become a newspaper proprietor, spreads Potterism abroad and finds that it is everywhere. It is Potterism and not Macaulayism which has enjoyed absolute power in the century of the Common Man. Rose describes it in her novel of the name as 'mainly an Anglo-Saxon disease. Worst of all in America, that great home of commerce, success and the booming of the second-rate'. Potterism is sentimental, anti-intellectual, fearful of the truth, dominated by the small-town or suburban conservative mentality. Mrs Thatcher, with her espousal of sub-Kiplingesque patriotism, lower-middle class commercial and moral values, and pro-American political views – both in the sense of pro-American foreign policy and the attempt to make England more like America with the abolition of the Welfare State and the belief that more shopping malls means more prosperity – Mrs Thatcher was the embodiment of Potterism. Rose would have hated her. Some of the reasons for that hatred would be frankly snobbish. But they would also be based on the belief that the values and levels of intelligence of Rose's sort are genuinely worth more than the values of Potterism.

In some of her books, her desire to distance herself from Potterism leads to an embarrassing sort of show-off cleverness which makes us uncomfortable, as when Daisy confronts a wild boar in *Keeping Up Appearances* and we are told by the narrator, 'Such a boar he seemed as was sent by an offended goddess to devastate Calydon or such a boar as Heracles pursued up Erymanthus, so fierce that he would require a hundred huntsmen to despatch him, with infinite sacrifice of life, or else Heracles with his noose.'

How this interrupts the narrative of what is supposed to be

an exciting scene! A young woman being chased by a wild boar, and Rose has to pause and remind us, as it were, that though she only had an *aegrotat* at Somerville, her father was a famous scholar, and she is cleverer than her own heroine, poor little Daisy.

In fact, of course, as readers of *Keeping Up Appearances* will remember, there is a deep division of personality in Daisy, who is timid, class-conscious and vulgar and Daphne, who wishes to be taken seriously by the Bloomsbury set. Daisy, like Rose, is someone who turns an honest penny writing nonsense for the Potterite press. Daphne, her suave cynical alter-ego, despises her for doing so. Re-reading these novels like *Potterism* and *Keeping Up Appearances* today, I am surprised by how little has changed in the world of the popular press. When the features editor of the *Sunday Wire* rings up Daisy – the date is 1928 – with an idea for an article, he sounds instantaneously recognisable.

> Look here, Miss Simpson. Can a woman run a baby and a business at the same time? Work out something on those lines. The editor wants it hot and live, to follow right on what Lady Lennox said about it at the Derby yesterday afternoon. Yes, she did: it's all in this morning's papers, with special headlines. Why? I don't know why. I suppose because it's about women and babies. Read it up, and get something out along those lines. Make it human. It doesn't matter which side you take, but make it live and human. Talk about the little chap, you know, as if he was there. Make 'em hear him crow.

No-one who has been employed by the Potter Press will fail to recognise this as the authentic voice of middle- to low-brow journalism.

Keeping Up Appearances, which is one of Rose's best novels, is, as I say, about a divided self. Daisy and Daphne are the same person. Daphne despises Daisy for her cowardice, for her low

social origins, for her lack of intellectual fibre. Daphne, like
innumerable Rose Macaulay heroines – many of whom have
sexless or male forenames like Stanley and Denham – positively
abominates any post-nineteenth-century explanations for the
psychological complexity of human character and in particular
rejects the Freudian view that sex is of great importance. On
her walk with Raymond, with whom she is in love, Daphne
discussed 'sex and its usually overestimated importance in the
life of man'. They agreed that much imaginative literature had
here struck a false note from all time. 'And now the pseudo-
scientists,' Raymond said, 'like Freud, poor old man, who's
hypnotized himself with observing diseased erotomaniacs and
thinking them normal till he can see nothing straight. . . . But
if you come to think of it, it's not really queer that anyone should
be sex-obsessed; it's rather queer that we're not all, considering
that we all originated from an impulse of sex emotion. It shows
how strong the other things must be.'

That's the unmistakable Rose Macaulay note, that last sentence! She was far too honest and sensible to think that there
was anything improper about the discussion of sexual matters.
But there were stronger things in life – the literature of the
ancients and of the seventeenth century, the love of family, the
love of God. While sophisticated Daphne is having her walks in
the wood with Raymond – and she is the side of Rose who liked
giving restaurant dinner parties which Virginia and Leonard
Woolf thought too smart, and chattering late into the night with
Morgan Forster or Raymond Mortimer – little Daisy is up to
something rather different. She has crept into Butterfield's mys-
terious and beautiful church of All Saints, Margaret Street. 'The
misty and incensed air crept about her, as she knelt with her
chin on her arms, staring through weary tears at the red sanctu-
ary light. Here was comfort and security. Something to hold to
in chaos. If not objective truth – and who was to know that? –
here to her was one kind of truth, shining like a lamp through

the falsehoods and entanglements of her uneasy and frightened life.'

Her most interesting writing could now be seen to be all about herself – that is something we must discuss in a minute. As a novelist, and as a journalist, she was sometimes too archly aware of her lack of experience of what Mr Potter would have called ordinary life. She must have been the author of the blurb of her novel *Staying with Relations*: 'She wrote this book largely as compensation for not having reached Guatemala.' The novel of course is set in Guatemala. 'All the things I had left undone,' she wrote once in an essay, 'crowded before my accusing conscience. I had not played mah-jongg, dyed the hair, worshipped in a Plymouth Brother's Chapel or a Jewish synagogue, visited the South Seas, the Zoo aquarium, Montmartre, Sheffield, Los Angeles, or Balham, injected cocaine, made a bead purse or a will, won money on a horse, found oil or gold, captured a flea, learnt Hebrew, Russian, American or Chinese, suffered an operation (save only on the teeth), stood for parliament, got married, adopted a child or a pet monkey, taken the veil . . .'

It was in 1925 she wrote that. Some of the same jokes – adopting a monkey – were to surface much later in her fiction. But what was she to write about? At one of the ever-recurrent London literary parties which she attended, Anthony Powell described to her the plot of a recent novel. She said at once, dismissively, that there could be no conceivable interest in a novel about adultery in Mayfair. She then retracted the remark at once, admitting that any subject was a suitable subject for fiction if it were handled with sufficient intelligence and interest. The mind slightly boggles at the thought of Rose having survived into our own day and turned the pages of a sex and shopping novel; but if the importance of the former subject in the life of man has been overestimated, she might have been interested, from an anthropological point of view, in the latter. I do not imagine that shopping played much part in her day-to-day existence. The domestic arts were not ones which she practised with much enthusiasm. A friend of hers told me – on what authority I do not know – that when she died no less than six unemptied teapots were discovered in her small flat. Her accounts in her published letters of a summer holiday spent with her beloved godchildren at a Butlin's holiday camp are delightful. Pliny the Younger spending a week among the plebs.

> Butlin's was quite fun; rather like a visit to the moon, quite out of this world. Absurd, of course, for an adult, but having the two children made it fun; they loved every minute of it. One unexpected thing was the little camp church, Angli-can, with a chaplain of great geniality to one and all; Mass every day at 7.30 and 8.30, to which I went (at 8.30), and it was very well attended. A radio voice announced each morning at 7.29, 'In one minute there will be a celebration of Holy Communion in the camp church.' Disgusted and sleepy voice from the chalet on my left, '*What* an entertain-ment!' We all slept in nice little chalets in a row, or rather in many rows, for there were about 500 campers at a time. We had swimming pools (but I bathed in the sea myself) and every kind of game and diversion, and my younger charge, who is pony-mad, rose every day and helped to groom the horses. There was a repertory company, which acted exciting dramas, and television, which I saw for the first time and didn't think much of. Why is it so popular? . . .
>
> I am still being bombarded with little Catholic Truth pamphlets, and long letters telling how I have no Mass, no sacraments, no priests. How rude they are! Imagine if I started writing in that vein to, say, Methodists. They are so stuck up and arrogant. Of course nothing *could* be so true as they think their Church is . . .

I am indebted to Miss Elizabeth Jenkins, herself an excellent novelist and a friend of Rose Macaulay, who writes to me as follows:

I have felt that for the last fifty years the most important development in novel-writing in our time is the rise of what I call the Reportage Novel, for lack of a better term: i.e. the novel which depends on a first-hand account of some profession, trade or occupation, efficiently underpinned by acute character-drawing, of course. There have been numerous instances of novels owing a great deal to first-hand descriptions of professional scenes – Mr Crosbie's office in *The Small House at Allington, Bleak House*, etc, but none where those descriptions were the be-all and end-all, with the simple but stunning exception of the one published in 1719, describing how you keep yourself alive on a desert island. But just before the last war there was an outbreak of them: *It's Cold in Front* by a taxi-driver, *Coming Sir* by a waiter, *Can I Help You? Madam*, by a dress-buyer in Fenwicks, and *I'm not Complaining* by a State schoolmistress are the ones I remember. Then, almost at once after the war, there was the great outburst – *One Pair of Feet* by Monica Dickens, *Doctor in the House* by Richard Gordon and *The Painswick Line* by Henry Cecil – hospital nursing, doctoring and the law all within a short space of each other and each one at the top of the tree! And of course the method has been going on ever since. Well, in the 1920s it had not been brought to light, but I remember, some time before 1930, hearing Rose lecture to a literary society in Cambridge on the novel and she obviously felt the lack of this unborn genre; she said, 'What I want to read about is the baker baking and the nun nunning.' Was that, in perspective, very interesting? It seems to show an intense, instinctive attraction towards a wide range of ordinary experience; not that she wasn't keenly, almost snobbishly, satirical – I've always treasured the exchange in *Catchwords and Claptrap* – Question: Would you like to know the meaning of the words you use? Answer: I do not suffer from the desire you mention.

It is not the only instance which could be cited of Rose's presci-ence – nose – for what was happening in modern fiction. Not, I think, that she was greatly interested in the modern novel. 'I do not put novels in my necessary shelves,' she once wrote in the *Listener*, 'with poetry, biography, letters, voyages, history diction-aries and essays.' The only novelists she habitually re-read were Jane Austen and E. M. Forster, a lifelong friend about whom she wrote a good book. However I remember that when I was asked by the Virago Press – how little Rose would have liked to have been published by something with this name – to write an introduction to *Told By An Idiot* – I was struck by the sentence in that novel: 'In 1790, 1690, 1590 and back through every decade of every century, there have been Rome Gardens, fastidi-ous, mondaine, urbane, lettered, critical, amused, sceptical and what was called in 1890 *fin de siècle*'. Rome Garden (who owes her curious first name to one of the phases when her father adopted Catholicism of the Latin variety) is a projection of a certain strand of Rose herself. But in her generalisation that there are certain constant figures in history, I felt that there was a germ of an idea which owed much to Virginia Woolf's *Orlando* – a book which we know Rose liked because she says in one of her letters that it is 'nonsense of course, but rather lovely and fascinating nonsense, don't you think?' I began to develop a theory that Rose Macaulay, having recently abandoned her Anglo-Catholic faith and discarded the poetic earnestness of her earlier novels, had found, in the last chapter of *Orlando*, the catalyst which enabled her to survey her lost certitudes with a voice appropriate to the moment. *Orlando* is a novel about an androgynous being who is a young man in the sixteenth century but by the twentieth century has turned into a woman. Rome, Stanley and Imogen in *Told By An Idiot* are all more or less sexless. Imogen, for example, was 'as sexless as any girl or boy may be. She was still in all her imaginings, her continuous unwritten stories about herself, a young man.' My theory of the debt owed by Rose Macaulay to Virginia Woolf rather collapsed when I looked up the dates of publication. *Told By An Idiot* was published in 1923. *Orlando* was published in 1928. If there is kinship between the two books – and I think there quite demonstrably is – then it was Mrs Woolf who owed a debt to Miss Macaulay and not the other way about.

One need hardly remind members of the London Library that Virginia Stephen was the child of just such an academic clerical dynasty as Rose herself. How we are to describe this class today I do not know. William Bodham Donne, who was London Librarian from 1852 to 1857, and who claimed descent from the poetical Dean of St Paul's, belonged to this class. John Wells in his history of the library makes this belle-lettrist member of the Apostles sound foppish, affected and unattractive. And with his fondness for France and French cooks and the theatre, he was not really a very good embodiment of the values of that class. The airs which he gave himself had so impressed themselves on the devoted housekeeper who looked after him in his widowhood that the clergyman who attended this woman's own deathbed remarked, 'It's no use talking to her of the glories of the Saints; she will only talk of the glory of the Donnes.'

Rose's letters to her cousin Hamilton Johnson, when they stray occasionally from their obsessively churchy themes, recall this lady. Johnson and Rose were both cousins of William Bodham Donne. They were cousins of practically everyone in that class – the Trevelyans, and the Conybeares, just as Virginia Woolf was related to a similar clutch of everybodies – the Thackerays, Julia Margaret Cameron and the Pattles, and so forth. These great dynasties, which provided this country with its

Masters of Trinity, and its London Librarians, and its Fellows of the Royal Society – as well as innumerable good minor writers, scholars, country parsons – could be said to be the backbone of England, the great educated class before education was available to all. To this class we owe nearly all the great social reforms of the nineteenth century, most of the best academics, lawyers, and clerics. With the death of this class – for it is now obsolete, dead as a dodo – we have coarser dons, fewer intelligent clergymen, and politicians who do not see the need either to speak in grammatical sentences or to put the greater good above the narrow interests of party or ambition.

I do not know how you would describe the class. Since it has vanished, it is not surprising that those who come in after days and look back upon this race of dinosaurs should get it wrong. I am sure that I do so myself. Rose's cousin John Cowper Powys is articulate in describing it. A member of this class would be literate and that would be the most important thing about her or him. A small private income would normally enable them to spend at least a few days each week with their books, whether or not they were professional clergymen or scholars. It was in a way the most important single fact about Rose that she belonged to this class, and had the leisure to read and to talk as much as she did, for the reading and the talk are what breathe through her novels and make them so distinctively what they are.

How astonished her contemporaries in the 1920s would be if they could discover how her reputation has faded since those days. The recent biography of Rose Macaulay by Jane Emery reminds us usefully of how extremely successful and popular Rose was. Those novels she wrote in the 1920s marked her out by critics as 'one of the most brilliant of living writers'. And so she was, so she was. But she has not lasted. The gallant attempts by publishers to put her into paperback sometimes only serve to remind us of how much she has dated. I have re-read most of her novels for the purpose of this lecture and I have enjoyed the experience. But it has not made me esteem her very highly as a novelist. The enjoyable, surprising things are the writings which concentrate upon her own vulnerability and her sense of the world as a strange, alien place. I want to talk a little about that in the remaining time. There is an essay she wrote on vagrants in 1925 called 'Beds and 'Omes' which makes good reading today in a city which contains so many people who live in tents and cardboard boxes. It is about a court case in which a man is had up for vagrancy. He has never been seen drunk. He earns his living as a casual farm labourer. And the Bench decrees that he should be sent down for seven days for vagrancy. Rose adds, 'Sleeping in a bed – it is, apparently of immense importance. Against those who sleep, from choice or necessity, elsewhere society feels righteously hostile. It is not done. . . . We have decided that the periods of rest which divide day from night shall be spent as a matter of regular routine, on mattresses between sheets and blankets.' There are still voluntary vagrants, though it would be a brave and insensitive man today who wrote Rose's essay. It is a good essay nonetheless, a celebration of the Outsider's last train home and having to ask the station master to unlock the station, and allow her to spend the night in the waiting room.

'If we were to keep the rooms unlocked at nights,' I was told, 'we should have all the ladies without 'omes coming in. That wouldn't be very nice.' All the ladies without 'omes. Pathetic, tragic picture. That night I was myself one of them, and knew exactly how cold they were, how 'omeless, how forlorn and weary, comforted only by the coffee stall at the corner of the street. Ladies without 'omes – gentlemen sleeping rough. Society has decreed that these ladies and gentlemen, on the chance nights when for some reason they do happen to want a bed or an 'ome should be denied these. They have forfeited their right.

In the novel which she wrote immediately after the War, *The World My Wilderness*, Rose Macaulay invented a young teenage heroine who is only at home in the ruined bomb-sites where, in a wonderful phrase, 'the shells of churches gaped like lost myths, and the jungle pressed in on them, seeking to cover them up'. It is the most raw and painful of her books. Like so many of her earlier novels, her protagonist is an awkward, lonely adolescent, unloved by her parents, alienated from the conventional world of grown-ups and their professions, haunted by a sense of sin and a sense of deep religious loneliness. Barbary's delinquency and lovelessness are written from the inside, which is such a surprising thing when we hear the accounts of what Rose looked like to her contemporaries when she was writing it – that gaunt, austere figure, on the verge of seventy years old when the book was published. Inside, as we know from the indiscretions of those whom she trusted to be more discreet, she was a heartbroken woman whose world was indeed a wilderness. The sex in *The World My Wilderness* – its casualness, and its association in Barbary's mind with death – are extraordinarily vivid. In my re-reading of the oeuvre this summer, I certainly put it very high – perhaps in some ways the best novel she wrote, but not the most enjoyable.

After she had finished it, as you know, she was commissioned by Thames and Hudson to write her book called *The Pleasure of Ruins*. I took it to Italy to read among the ruins of Paestum and Herculaneum, and I am bound to say I was disappointed. It reeks of the London Library. She has been into the Library and taken out an armful of eighteenth-century travellers one week, an armful of poets the next, and although her comments are urbane and witty, and the passages from a wide range of writers are well-chosen, there is something arch and unworked-out about the book. But we can be grateful she wrote it, because it was in the course of travelling about the Mediterranean in pursuit of ruins that she had that tantalising glimpse of the Towers of Trebizond.

Father Gerard Irvine, a close friend in latter days, was once having a conversation with Rose about *Brideshead Revisited*. An absurd book, Rose said – how I agree with her – about a Roman Catholic family, persecuted by Queen Elizabeth and holding fast to their faith and all going to the bad. Absurd book. She said she rather thought of writing a sort of counterblast to *Brideshead Revisited*. It would be about an Anglican family who had been persecuted by Bloody Mary and Oliver Cromwell and still kept the faith, and unlike Evelyn Waugh's characters who all seem to go to the bad, Rose's Anglicans would go to the good. She had thought of a title: *Maidenhead Retained*. And the narrator of *The Towers of Trezibond* tells us:

> We belong to an old Anglican family, which suffered under the penal laws of Henry VII, Mary I and Oliver C. Under Henry VIII we did indeed acquire and domesticate a dissolved abbey in Sussex, but were burned, some of us, for refusing to accept the Six Points; under Mary we were again burned, naturally, for heresy; under Elizabeth we dug ourselves firmly into Anglican life, compelling our Puritan tenants to dance round maypoles and revel at Christmas and informing the magistrates that Jesuit priests had concealed themselves in the chimney pieces of our Popish neighbours.

From the first magnificent sentence – '"Take my camel, dear," said my Aunt Dot as she climbed down from this animal on her return from High Mass' – to the last, Rose Macaulay is completely in control. And certain, artistically, of what she is doing. And able, therefore, as she must have done in her conversation, to vacillate between frivolity and high seriousness. And its theme is no less than that of *Brideshead* as described by Evelyn Waugh – the operation of divine grace. Ivy Compton-Burnett regretted

Rose Macaulay's return to the church in the last five years of her life and wondered why she could not be 'a perfectly sound agnostic like everybody else'. The reasons lay buried in childhood, when she would retreat from her large family and climb a tree in order to read *The Imitation of Christ*. Throughout her long love affair with the Christian religion – either as a practising Anglican or as what she called an Anglo-agnostic – she was haunted by the big questions. We find her preoccupation characteristically expressed in an essay which she wrote after – like poor Papa in *Told By An Idiot* – she had 'lost her faith again':

> Strange indeed, that this odd, flying fragment we call earth, spinning so crazily, so precariously in space, like a child's ball on a string, that may at any moment break loose and fly off at a tangent into illimitable space, to meet at last a horrid end in the fiery maw of some monstrous devouring sun – strange that this irresponsible unwholesome ellipse originating who knows how, bound none knows whither, breaking all over its surface into fetid vegetation and horrid, gelatinous life, life running on myriads of legs on four, on two, on none, should have broken also into this infinitely paradoxical life of the spirit. Man, in the beginning, a gluttonous, self-preserving, unethical protoplasm, living plain and thinking plainer, has somehow, in the course of his quest for higher living, found higher thinking too, and that most strange apprehension that we call a sense of ethics. No amount of investigation into the origins of moral ideas, no amount of discovery that they are, one and all, utilitarian in basis, evolving out of the tribal sense of the welfare of the community will really explain this thing.

It is in the struggle of good and evil in her own life – a happy but guilt-ridden adulterous affair – that the narrator of *The Towers of Trebizond* confronts these matters and reacquaints herself with the confused but inspiring heritage of Christendom. Visiting the Church of the Holy Sepulchre in Jerusalem with her mother, Laurie contemplates the wickedness and bloodshed and cruelty which it represents:

> And this failure of the Christian Church, of every branch of it in every country, is one of the saddest things that has happened in all the world. But it is what happens when a magnificent idea has to be worked out by human beings who do not understand much of it but interpret it in their own way and think they are guided by God, whom they have not yet grasped. And yet they have grasped something, so that the Church has always had greater magnificence and much courage, and people have died for it in agony, which is supposed to balance all the other people who have had to die in agony because they did not accept it, and it has flowered up in learning and culture and beauty and art, to set against its darkness and incivility and obscurantism and barbarity and nonsense, and it has produced saints and martyrs and kindness and goodness, though they have also freely occurred outside it, and it is a wonderful and most extraordinary pageant of contradictions, and I, at least, want to be inside it, though it is a foolishness to most of my friends.

The Towers of Trebizond is not really a novel; more an essay on this theme; but it works, it is the most successful, artistically, of all her books; I suppose because, in old age, she felt she could be most freely herself. Anglicanism, which is going through rather a rocky patch at the moment, had a notable flowering in the middle years of this century; and so many of its most attractive exponents were not clergymen but lay people – T. S. Eliot, W. H. Auden, John Piper, Dorothy L. Sayers, above all perhaps John Betjeman and Rose Macaulay. Their camp, churchy jokes, and their mildly obsessive (though perfectly understandable) dislike of Roman Catholicism cannot perhaps bear endless repetition today. But they stood for something good, and gentle and strong – strong enough to admit of its own doubts about itself, strong enough to be unashamedly aesthetic. The mingling of humour and seriousness is one of its great characteristics. Among all the jokes about being High, there is a profound awareness of life's seriousness, of the human need to lead a 'life of the spirit' or to die. So Father Hugh Chantry Pigg, a ludicrous figure who, with Aunt Dot's assistance, is trying to convert the Turks to High Anglicanism, is also the mouthpiece of the most searching moral and spiritual crisis of Laurie's life. In a rather similar way, the element of Rose Macaulay's character which provided friends with some of their tallest and funniest stories about her – her bad driving – is the means in this story of tragedy, in which Laurie inadvertently kills the man she loves and thereby feels imprisoned in a sort of hell. 'Someone once said that hell would be or now is, living without God and with evil, and being unable to get used to it. God is leaving us alone for ever; we have driven ourselves out, we have lost God and gained hell. I now live in two hells, for I have lost God and live also without love, or without the love I want, and I cannot get used to that either.' The effectiveness of the novel as a Christian statement is so much stronger because Laurie is left outside the church at the end, though one senses that, like the author, she will eventually move towards the Towers of Trebizond and find herself at home after all.

Perhaps it was a miracle, that though she was so frequently up before the beak for dangerous driving, she never did in fact kill anyone. I like the description by Compton Mackenzie of being given a lift by Rose and becoming so terrified that he asked her to stop and let him out of the car. She swerved to a halt on the wrong side of the road and, 'as I hastily got out I see now Rose Macaulay sweeping on southward in a series of ample zig-zags'.

What survives of her can perhaps be best described as a voice. The memorable parts of her novels are not the characters or the plots but the long, frenetic sentences of well-tuned, jokey-serious talk. She disliked her early novels so much that she tried to steal them from the shelves of the London Library lest they be read by her friends. At her best, she could be described as a novelist of ideas, and she would probably have understood why Nicholas Mosley resigned from the Booker panel this year. Like the great Russian novelists, she used her books chiefly as vehicles for discussing the unanswerable questions which she asked herself as she hurtled down her zig-zag path from faith to doubt to faith, and tormented all the time by the great adventure of love and guilt. I can see why her friends and acquaintances felt so desolated when she died, for there is no-one quite like her, and one suspects that there will never be anyone quite like her again. I used to be an addict of her novels and essays, and though I cannot recapture the first fine careless rapture of reading her for the first time, I feel such gratitude to her not only for her books but for the 'personal pleasures' which she opened up for me when I first read them. *They Were Defeated* now reads to me like *The Constant Nymph* replayed as a costume drama, but it was through reading that book that I discovered the seventeenth-century poets. Likewise, it was through reading *The World My Wilderness* that I, a provincial, discovered the romance of walking in London. *The Towers of Trebizond* was – is – something much more to me than a novel. Even the letters – which she so earnestly asked their clerical recipient to destroy – and whose publication was really a breach of the seal of the confessional – have played an important role in my own life of the spirit. I remember as a very young man talking of Rose Macaulay to Elizabeth Bowen, and asking her opinion of the letters. Inhaling deeply from her untipped cigarette, Miss Bowen said, 'I'm a s-sort of Christian, but it appals me to think of R-rose feeling she had to apologise for a love affair to that r-r-rat-faced priest.' But then she added, 'You are a different generation and I dare say it is all right for you to read the letters.' I think she is right, and I cannot regret having read them. They bring her so vividly to life. I wish I had known her. I loved her so much, not only as a writer but as the friend I'd never had that I named my first child after her. I envy the generation of David Wright, who wrote that 'during the last war one of the famous sights of London, a peripatetic phenomenon usually seen chained to the railings of the London Library, was a lady's bicycle, angular, battered, with a wickerwork basket strapped to the handlebars and boldly inscribed on the frame in white paint, the name ROSE MACAULAY.'

SOME PREVIOUS LIBRARIANS

JOHN WELLS

Sir Charles Hagberg Wright

SOME PREVIOUS
LIBRARIANS

'REMEMBER we are not offering laurel crowns and the Bank of England, but hard work and one hundred and fifty pounds a year.' Carlyle, for once, was being realistic, and he was writing about the job of Librarian at the London Library. 'Perfection is a thing we must not look for!'

This did not stop him flying into a rage when more temperate friends suggested that his young right-hand man in founding the Library, the lawyer William Dougal Christie, should stay on as Secretary, and that the post of Librarian should be occupied, at least until they could all see what kind of man they really wanted, by a clerk.

'It is like sending out a military expedition for conquest of foreign countries under a *serjeant*, with strict provision that *when* he has made conquests, we will send a General!'

There is no more telling proof of Carlyle's capacities as prophet and seer. In a single military simile he was defining the eternal dilemma of members and their representative committee for the rest of the Library's existence. The Librarian could not be a mere non-commissioned officer, incapable of taking the initiative, nor, as Carlyle seems to have realised within moments of writing the word 'General', could he be a holy terror of whom members and committee went in mortal dread. He had had enough of that with Panizzi at the British Museum.

He therefore devised a second more theological definition, his agony of soul expressed by those bird's-claw semi-colons that punctuate his thought on paper.

> My notion of the Librarian's function does not imply that he shall be king over us; nay, that he shall ever quit the address and manner of a *servant* to the Library; but he will be a *wise* servant, watchful and diligent, discerning what is what, incessantly endeavouring, *rough-hewing* all things for us; and under the guise of a wise servant, *ruling* actually while he serves. He should be like a nobleman's steward.

This from a man who was not looking for perfection.

The objection to his own favourite candidate, Cochrane, was that at fifty-nine he was too old, and Christie found him 'inert'. Carlyle himself admitted to having detected what he called 'a shade of obstinacy in him', but the alternative was 'guidableness', and 'guidableness' meant lack of initiative.

'The *guidablest* of all quadrupeds is a starved cadger's garron' – Carlyle's quaint old Scots term for a broken-down horse – 'reduced to skin and bone; no kicking or plunging in him; but alas, withal there is no *go* in him.' Cochrane, he believed, whatever Christie said, had '*go*'.

Carlyle, like every other subsequent member of the Library, certainly felt like a nobleman: but the term 'nobleman's steward' seems to have been written in the knowledge that it might be seen by the Librarian. The horse image, regrettably, recurs. When he told the acting Secretary, Brittan, who had supervised the initial collection of books, that his services would no longer be required after the Library opened, he was, according to Carlyle, 'very pettish'. 'I had to fling the reins on his neck and tell him he was free to go.'

In considering the first four Librarians, then – Cochrane, Bodham Donne, Harrison and Hagberg Wright, who span almost exactly the first century of the London Library's existence, from Cochrane's appointment in March 1841 to Hagberg

Wright's death in harness in February 1940 – I have done my best to get my information, as it were, from the horse's mouth.

In writing the history of the Library I was indebted to Miron Grindea, whose special issue of *Adam* devoted to recollections about the Library, including Hagberg Wright's essay *The Soul's Dispensary*, was published in hardback in 1978. It was he who introduced me to Antony Farrell's invaluable research on the earlier London Library founded in 1785.

I never met the fifth Librarian, Christopher Purnell, Hagberg's deputy who carried on until 1950, though I met his son and spoke to his daughter. But among living witnesses I received by far the most help from Simon Nowell-Smith, Librarian from 1950 until 1954, and from Stanley Gillam who retired in 1980, who made available to me his notes about the early committee meetings in Cochrane's time. I have already acknowledged my debt to Joan Bailey, champion of the staff. I need hardly add that the history of the Library could not have been written, and would have been no fun at all to write, without the help and jokes and constant enthusiasm of the present Librarian, Douglas Matthews.

It was Simon Nowell-Smith who told me one story about Mr Cox that for some reason did not find its way into *Rude Words*. Cox took against one of Nowell-Smith's friends, a member of the Library called Comyns-Carr, and affected to ignore him. When he did deign to address him he would call him 'Mr Wilkinson'. Nowell-Smith took Cox on one side, explaining that his friend's name was Comyns-Carr, and the old boy appeared to accept this. The next time Comyns-Carr approached the Issue Desk Cox again boomed 'Mornin', Mr Wilkinson!' Comyns-Carr lost his temper, and hissed, 'My name is not Wilkinson, it is Comyns-Carr!' Cox looked up, blinked behind his spectacles, and said, 'Oh! *Changed* it, 'ave yer?'

Cox, admittedly, was never Librarian, even though he figures in the Suggestions Book in the course of the Great Tearoom

Debate as 'the Librarian in the thirties who provided not only tea, but also buttered toast'; but he represents the staff militant, just as Cochrane's assistant, John Edward Jones, who was passed over as Librarian by both Bodham Donne and Harrison, represents the staff frustrated but still doggedly loyal to the institution.

In the course of preparing this paper I have uncovered some fresh evidence about each of the four librarians, which I hope will be of interest in understanding them better.

*   *   *

My key witness against Cochrane was Jane Carlyle: visiting the Library in September 1847, not admittedly in the best of moods, to borrow *Vanity Fair*, she observed that the books were too filthy to handle, 'officials mortal drunk or worse'. When she complained, she said, she was asked, 'Are you aware, ma'am, of the death of Mrs Cochrane?' Had Cochrane, like the rest of the staff, taken to the bottle? My first doubts came recently, when I discovered that Mrs Cochrane was still alive at the time of Cochrane's death, asking for a fortnight's grace to move her furniture out of the Librarian's flat on the top floor of Beauchamp House.

According to Christie and others, Cochrane turned out not to have 'go'. When he did take initiative, making some kind of private deal to buy books for the Library from Whitaker's, he was censured by the Committee. While he remained Librarian, it is true, Carlyle defended him, praising his helpfulness, good-nature, patience and cheerfulness.

But after his death even Carlyle had to admit that 'poor Cochrane', as he called him, had been 'indolent'. 'He did much really useful work in a quiet lucid way, in spite of his indolence, and for practical help as a bibliographer he was by far the best I ever met with in this country. True, he by no means shone as a distributor of books, and could never bring himself to believe that the wish of everybody without restraint to anybody could not be complied with.'

A glance at the Library's records of borrowings for the first few months will confirm this view. Books are signed out by proxy or not signed out at all, some are marked as returned with an 'R' on the issue slip, some merely scored through with a stroke of the pen.

The general outline of Cochrane's career will be already familiar. John George Cochrane was a Glasgow man, the son of a lawyer who gave him what he called 'a fair education', without sending him to university, and found him a job, probably in publishing, though he may simply have been apprenticed to a bookseller. He came south to London in the year 1800, at the age of nineteen, determined to make his fortune.

Within ten years he was able to found a firm in Fleet Street, White, Cochrane and Co., and much was made of the fact, at the time of his applying to the Library, that White, Cochrane and Co. had gone bankrupt after only two years. Cochrane's response to this bankruptcy was a pamphlet, his only published work, *The Case stated between the Public Libraries and the Booksellers*, printed in 1813. It is a remarkably lucid and entertaining history of the Copyright Laws, condemning as ridiculous the provision that every publisher, however expensive the book he published, and in however many volumes it might appear, was obliged to supply eleven copies free of charge. One went to the British Museum, others to various university libraries. Of these the one that really stuck in Cochrane's throat was Cambridge. Cambridge, he said, was making enough money out of publishing work by its own graduates to be able to afford to pay for books brought out by struggling independent publishers.

Cochrane then spent the years after Waterloo working for a German bookseller in Soho Square, Treuttel, Wuerz, Treuttel Junior and Richter. In the 1820s Richter began to publish *The*

Foreign Quarterly Review, and Cochrane was made its full-time editor. This lasted for seven years. Richter went bankrupt, and Cochrane published the last issue, for December 1834, at his own expense.

Over fifty but still ambitious, he revived it the following year as *Cochrane's Foreign Quarterly Review*. It lasted for two issues and then folded.

He subsequently applied without success for the Librarianship of the Advocates' Library and the Signet Library, both in Edinburgh. Instead, he catalogued Sir Walter Scott's Library at Abbotsford. When he was recommended to Carlyle, he was editing a local newspaper in Hereford. A career, it seemed, that might have driven any man to drink.

I have only recently come across several letters from Cochrane in the manuscript collection of the British Library which go some way to filling in that outline. In one letter he remembers the early years of the century he spent as a book-dealer in Fleet Street, attending sales at a time when prices were suddenly climbing – 'thus the hammer vibrates,' he quotes his friend Thomas Dibdin in a book called *Bibliomania*, 'after a bidding of FORTY POUNDS, where formerly it used regularly to fall at FOUR', drawing up catalogues and finding books for friends and patrons.

Cochrane, it is clear, was always more than a bookseller. In 1811 he sent his friend Philip Bliss, under-librarian at what Cochrane calls 'your Bod', a present of a new edition of Fuller's *Worthies* – 'To save you the trouble of cutting up the leaves I have had it bound' – and thanking Bliss for his interest in their new publishing company. 'I consider I have done everything I can do with propriety. If we are successful I shall be very happy and very proud, if otherwise I shall not grieve to death.' It is an attitude more appropriate to a gentleman of letters than an aspiring businessman.

White, Cochrane published what would nowadays be considered an ambitious list, expensively illustrated books that included Sowerby's *English Botany* and Lambert's treatise on Varieties of Pine. The firm went under in the same slump that engulfed Walter Scott's publishers, Archibald Constable, and it is worth noting that Cochrane's great friend was Constable's partner, Robert Cadell.

Constable was known to be 'lavish and enterprising to rashness', Cadell, Cochrane's friend, 'cautious and frugal', and it was Walter Scott himself who said when the partnership dissolved that 'Constable without Cadell was like getting the clock without the pendulum, the one having the ingenuity, the other the caution of the business.'

After the publication of his pamphlet on copyright, Cochrane went before a select committee at the House of Commons, which appears to have agreed with him, and over twenty years later Parliament officially reduced the number of free copies from eleven to five. Too late admittedly for White, Cochrane and Co., but nonetheless a moral victory.

In 1814, in the wake of his bankruptcy, Cochrane is apologising to Philip Bliss for having 'quite forgot' to look up the plays of the seventeenth-century dramatist Arthur Wilson in the Stationers' Register. He has found an entry for 4 September 1646, with a list of over forty plays registered by Mr Robinson and Mr Mozeley, the last of which are *Switzer* and *The Corporal*, both by Dr Wilson, and a subsequent long list registered in September 1653 including *The Inconstant Lady* by the same author. 'I paid a shilling for the search,' he concludes, 'and am, dear Bliss, most truly yours, J. G. Cochrane.' Easy enough to see why Carlyle should have been so keen to engage him as the first Librarian.

In 1815 there is the nearest thing to a quarrel over money with Bliss about the payment of £1.13.0 for a book Cochrane had bought for him in the Gordonstoun sale. There are also uncharacteristic slurred loops in Cochrane's handwriting in this letter that might lend support to Jane Carlyle's theory.

His next encounter with Bliss came when they both applied for the job of librarian at the Advocates' Library. They did not meet or correspond, but Bliss got the job. It was Cadell, Cochrane's publisher friend, who asked him instead to catalogue Walter Scott's library at Abbotsford. He stayed for five months. He was disappointed to find 'so few works of rarity or curiosity in the collection.' 'As a *whole*, it is *respectable* for a private gentleman, but that is as much as can be said for it. Sir Walter was evidently not a true *bibliomaniac*.'

Then, after nearly twenty years' silence, he wrote to Bliss asking for a testimonial. He was about to apply for the job of librarian at the Signet Library in Edinburgh. They had known each other, he said, for over thirty years. 'Fortune,' he wrote, 'has not hitherto smiled upon any outliners to woo her.' If, however, he succeeded in obtaining the prize he was now contending for, he would be, as he put it, 'perfectly satisfied to forget the rebuffs I have hitherto met with'.

He was not elected, and in December 1840 he wrote to Bliss again from Hereford, where he was recovering from Fortune's last rebuff. He encloses the fullest list in existence, thirty-two names, of the full founding committee of the London Library, and asks Bliss to write to anyone on it he knows. 'As the number of electors is so small, and the metropolis is a field where I am better known than I was at Edinburgh, I flatter myself that my chances of success are greater. *Four* of the members of the committee are my personal friends, and have promised me their support.'

These, by process of elimination, seem to have been Carlyle, George Lewis, Forster and Dickens. His opponent, Baynes, had, he knew, the support of the Headmaster of Harrow and of what Cochrane calls 'a knot of Cambridge men' – the first positive identification of the Apostles at work.

Baynes got eight votes, Cochrane eleven. What became of the other thirteen members of the founding Committee on that crucial afternoon is not recorded.

Cochrane may have been indolent, but he exercised as much authority as any Librarian that followed him. It was Cochrane, not the Chairman, who wrote to Monckton Milnes telling him that the Committee would in future be reduced to twelve, Cochrane who signed the lease with Pusey for 49 Pall Mall, Cochrane who appeared in court to argue with the Clerk of the Parish that a library run exclusively for the pursuit of learning and with so many distinguished and eminent members should not pay rates, Cochrane who recommended the acquisition of St James's Square, suggested the room overlooking the square should be the Reading Room and agreed to find a new fireplace. It was also Cochrane who, in four days, in November 1845, moved 20,000 books, with the help of John Edward Jones, into what he called 'our new and permanent domicile'.

I imagine Cochrane then as a tall, white-haired, slightly stooping old Scot with yellowing teeth, his head held slightly to one side. What did he feel about the Librarianship, as he stood on the partitioned-off landing by the coathooks on the first floor of the old gambling house in Pall Mall for the last time on that cold winter's morning, keys in hand, turning to go downstairs and say goodbye to his old friends at Charles and Henry Senior, Foreign Booksellers, smelling for the last time the smell of new leather from John Martin the bootmakers, and even tempted perhaps by the dark fruitier smell of claret from Bell, Rannie and Co., the wine merchants who also shared the ground floor? That for a true *bibliomaniac*, I like to imagine, fortune had at last smiled on him.

*   *   *

His successor Bodham Donne, it must be remembered, was elected after the epic battle in committee when Carlyle inflicted a crushing defeat on Gladstone, who was trying to introduce as Librarian his Italian protégé Mr Lacaita, arrived from Italy only four months earlier. Any fears that Lacaita, though a demented snob, might have made even a tolerably intelligent Librarian will be allayed by reading his own account of being briefly imprisoned in Naples. Trying to communicate with the priest in the next room he devised a code, one knock for A, two for B, three for C and twenty-six for Z. He said it took him five minutes to tap out 'Com' esta?', and God only knows how long to get an answer.

The necessary closing of ranks against Lacaita, though, excluded John Edward Jones, assured by the Carlyles that he was their candidate, and led to the election of William Bodham Donne. Even Carlyle, who voted for him, may have been unaware that Bodham Donne was an Apostle, a friend and contemporary of the 'knot of Cambridge men' on the committee.

The son of an eccentric Norfolk squire who kept a pet duck, William Bodham Donne was recommended to Charles Lamb as a child of great promise. He never met Lamb, but after a sickly childhood which meant him being taught at home he went to the King Edward VI School at Bury St Edmunds with three other future Apostles, Edward Fitzgerald, translator of Omar Khayyam, James Spedding, editor of Bacon, and John Kemble, son of the actor Charles and sister of the actress Fanny Kemble.

Under the influence of F. D. Maurice at Cambridge, Donne refused to take a degree, a protest against the rule that all graduates must subscribe to the Thirty-Nine Articles. He married, produced five children, and in his late thirties two slim volumes, one about magic and witchcraft and one, *Old Roads and New Roads*, contrasting the winding ways of old with the straight new railroads.

His wife died suddenly, soon after the birth of their youngest child, but he seemed on the available evidence to be a man who had, as Carlyle might have put it, 'puddled away his time' in Norfolk until 1852, when at the age of forty he rather lackadaisically took his first job as Librarian of the London Library.

His real passion was the theatre, and after offering to deputise for the Examiner of Plays, his old friend John Kemble, when he went to Germany he took over the position full-time on Kemble's death in 1857 and resigned from the Librarianship.

He was, it seems, unbelievably grand: he was related, he said, to the poet Donne, and the Bodhams had the money. He gave elegant little dinner parties in the Librarian's flat in the attic, which he termed his 'precipice', with food brought in from a French caterer in the Opera Arcade. He was worshipped by his housekeeper, Mary Trollope, who in wet weather clattered across St James's Square on pattens to shop at Covent Garden, and who once told Lord Derby's butler, when he offered to show her the table laid for a Cabinet Dinner at Number 10 Downing Street, 'That's nothing to what we have at Mr Donne's.'

He was also infuriatingly affected. My witness here is Fanny Kemble, with whom he kept up a brittle correspondence, flashing with *bons mots* and Latin tags. 'My wit, like Iago's, acts like bird-lime, it plucks out brains and all (*voici mon apologue*).'

Not surprisingly, he found writing a strain. 'As I grow old I become more fastidious in my composition. I never had, nor ever shall have, the "pen of a ready writer".'

Bodham Donne seemed to find everything a strain, and particularly the Librarianship. 'I believe people think I have a light place. I wish they could try it for a week.' There were letters to write, complaints to be dealt with, literary questions to answer, accounts to settle and the catalogue to be kept up to date. His talk of seven hours' work, from eleven to six, which he claimed 'rather took the freshness out of one', is probably in his case an exaggeration.

Hagberg Wright, who looked over the accounts in Bodham Donne's day, said that his Cambridge supporters 'were perhaps too kind in calling him "a Man of Business"'. As to dispensing advice to the members, John Edward Jones told Jane Carlyle, if we can trust a word she said, that Bodham Donne never came out of the Librarian's Room at the back of the building. He was indeed summoned by the committee in 1853 to answer a great many complaints from members.

Again, fresh evidence, from a bundle of family correspondence in a cupboard at the London Library, suggests that he was not altogether the self-obsessed belle-lettriste he appears in his correspondence with Fanny Kemble. His reason for staying at home after his wife's death was to look after his sons until they were old enough to go to the university. When John Kemble went to Germany, with very little money and escaping an estranged wife who lived in the country and had become an alcoholic, Bodham Donne did Kemble's job and sent him the salary.

He was not a good Librarian. He was never, like Cochrane, a true *bibliomaniac*, and his attitude to the members left a lot to be desired. In 1857, when he left, Lacaita was again proposed as a possible successor. Bodham Donne wrote to a mutual acquaintance to say that he was sure Lacaita would be ideal, and would get on splendidly with the committee.

> That is the *couleur de rose* side of the matter: there are, however, less pleasant circumstances between some of the *members* and the Secretary, which may make a *gentleman* pause before accepting an office in all other respects agreeable. I doubt whether I could much longer have put up with the almost daily provocations to *explode*, which the unreasonableness of many, the unpunctuality of many, and the utter want of civility in some, tend to excite. I should be sorry that an accomplished and refined gentleman like Mr Lacaita should take the post under the delusion that he will have in it either much leisure for his own pursuits or much peace of mind in his public duties.

The members, too, had probably had enough of Donne. He himself describes Charles Reade, author of *The Cloister and the*

Hearth, sitting in the Librarian's Room looking at him with his head on one side, 'deriving seemingly much amusement from the contemplation. He may think of turning me into the *père respectable* of a romance.'

A photograph of Bodham Donne survives. He has a high forehead, wears a silk bow, and presses his lips together in a witty smile. In August 1856 he was writing in his back room in St James's Square, knowing that all his friends were out of town for the summer, faced with the task, he claimed, of cataloguing 80,000 books.

Fanny Kemble in Boston, Massachusetts, couldn't believe there really were so many. 'Yes, the London Library *does* contain 80,000 books, and I am the luckless wight whose duty it is to sort and give an account of those same.'

Was he, as a Librarian, entirely without any saving grace? Perhaps not. No man who wrote about witchcraft and roads, and who wrote about them so discursively, can have been wholly out of sympathy with the Library. I like to imagine him on that hot August afternoon getting up from his half-completed *bons mots* to Fanny Kemble, and from his altogether unstarted work on the London Library catalogue, and taking down his own book *Old Roads and New Roads,* the fruit in itself of so much idle roaming along bookshelves. There, among his appalling digressions down so many what he would I am sure have termed *culs de sac,* he might have found, as the smell of horse manure drifted in through the open window from Fortnum and Masons' stables, a single good joke about the innkeeper in Wales who replaced the sign of the cockerel outside his pub with a portrait of the Bishop of Llandaff. Not surprisingly regular drinkers decided to go elsewhere, so the innkeeper added a caption under the Bishop's picture on the signboard, '*This is the Old Cock*'.

*

Cochrane had served for eleven years, Bodham Donne for five. Robert Harrison who came next, in 1857, remained Librarian for thirty-five years. He was chosen in reaction to Bodham Donne's dilettantism, as the first professional Librarian, subsequently the founder of the Library Association of Great Britain. He had begun work in a bookshop in High Holborn, worked as tutor to an aristocratic family in Russia, and wrote a memoir when he got back dedicated to A. H. Layard, *Notes of a Nine Years' Residence in Russia*.

Russia seems to have changed very little in the hundred years that followed: he was spied on, and complains of 'the moral lethargy, the insidious torpor, of being conscious all the time of some invisible controlling powers'. The English certainly have changed: in those days English people who went to Russia could speak Russian, and Harrison complains of the Russians' bad manners in accosting Mrs Harrison on a bus, asking her how old she was, what her husband did, and how much he earned a year.

He returned to be Librarian of the Leeds Library. According to his testimonials – and this may have been the line that won him the appointment as successor to Bodham Donne – he had found the Library in Leeds 'in great confusion', and had introduced 'very satisfactory arrangements'.

A Liverpudlian by birth, he described his father as a 'gentleman in easy circumstances' who was touring the Continent with his young wife at the end of the Napoleonic wars, so that their eldest son William was born in Amiens. He returned to Liverpool, sank all his money in a brewery which went bankrupt, leaving his wife Mary Harrison, daughter of a prosperous hat manufacturer in Stockport, to support them and educate three sons.

Miraculously she did so by painting watercolours – 'a branch of blackberry blossom lying near a bird's nest, delightful groups of violets, cowslips, and the most beautiful roses.' She moved to

London, probably to Hampstead, when Robert was eleven, and died at the age of eighty-eight having completed her pictures for that year's exhibition.

Robert's two older brothers, William and George, were both watercolourists. George died young, having studied under Constable, and William, who painted in his spare time, worked all his life at the Bank of England.

These facts are to be found, surprisingly enough, in the *Dictionary of National Biography*. Harrison, at the end of his time at the Library, was persuaded by the editor, Leslie Stephen, to write nearly ninety entries, all fairly run-of-the-mill subjects at the beginning of the alphabet, as a reward for which Leslie Stephen allowed him to include his mother and two brothers.

Harrison, as I have explained at greater length elsewhere, began his career at the London Library full of admiration for the members, keeping a rough and ready record of his conversations with them in a carriage arrears book drawn up by poor John Edward Jones, still Assistant Librarian, and filled with Jones's flowing copperpate.

The antipathy between Harrison and Jones was commented on by Bodham Donne, who continued to come in to the Library, and as if in answer to Jones's mute complaint, Harrison has written on the flyleaf of the carriage arrears book, 'I have taken this book for my own scrawling, because it is no longer of use for anything else.'

In this notebook he rarely writes about his own feelings, and when he does reveals at first a rather naïve and Pooter-like nature. Has he influenced world events by the odd word to a Minister about the American Civil War or the Crimea? He seems a conventional, church-going man, amused and sometimes a little shocked by the Positivists but tolerant of the goings-on of adulterous members like George Lewes and Mary Anne Evans. He was also not without a rather lugubrious sense of humour.

Jane Carlyle talked to him about her husband's sensitivity to train whistles from across the river, and how she had considered making him ear-plugs.

> Going on to speak of deaf people and their trumpets, she said that Harriet Martineau used one at their house one day. Carlyle was talking to her while suffering from a cold which made the water run from his nose. Mrs C. amused herself by watching the trickling stream, and by speculating on the effect of a drop getting into the trumpet. If it reached the tympanum of the listener the effect, she thought, would be something like the crack of doom.

Harrison was always fascinated by medical details, as he was when Thackeray told him how he mastered his bilious attacks with calomel, and when poor Bryan Hunt shot himself.

Many of the conversations like that with Jane Carlyle take place in the Librarian's room, but the majority are odd remarks members made while he was helping them to look for books. That he was appreciated in the early years is clear from his account of the time he and his son Bo were on holiday in Wiltshire in wet weather, and were asked to Wilton for lunch, where they met not only Gladstone who was staying then, but also Monckton Milnes and the first woman to be a life member of the Library, the best-looking ugly woman Monckton Milnes had ever seen, Carlyle's bright goddess Lady Ashburton.

He even shared something of Cochrane's passion for books, and newspaper advertisements for some very odd rarities are glued into the notebook. '*Mémoires de Mademoiselle de Montpensier, Fille de Gaston d'Orleans* 8 vols wanting vol 2 1746 (3/6d would be worth 12/- if complete) Mademoiselle used to say she did not utter falsehoods, but she supplied by the exercise of her imagination the defects of her memory.'

Bryan Hunt shot himself when Harrison had been at St James's Square for nearly twenty years, and things seem to have been jogging along. Admittedly, when a pistol was discharged in the Periodicals Room upstairs nobody actually did anything. But as I have explained elsewhere, the old house was so padded and soundproofed with books that is not entirely surprising.

Carlyle, you remember, was talking to Harrison in the Librarian's Room, waiting for the Second Volume of Motley's *Rise of the Dutch Republic* to be brought to him, and it was Jones, on duty in the Reading Room, who had to step over the convulsive suicide to get it down from its shelf.

Harrison, from his photographs in later life, was a stocky, heavy-featured man in a velvet-collared coat with a resolute set to his mouth. We can imagine him most clearly attending to Gladstone in the Reading Room, two detectives waiting outside on the landing, as he helped the great man find the original of a Latin quotation he has repeated from memory, hampered by the attentions of an over-zealous Eton master, and wondering at how vastly superior Gladstone's line was to the original.

He enjoyed Carlyle's friendship and some degree of intimacy – Carlyle told him after Jane died, 'It is as though I had lost my skin, she was everything to my comfort' – and Carlyle seemed to think that for all its faults the Library under Harrison was 'some average approximation what I hoped.'

But had Carlyle or the committee taken a more active interest they might have detected an even more marked strain of obstinacy in him than they had detected in Cochrane, the same strain of native independence that made life unbearable for him in Russia.

When Harrison called the first meeting of what was to become the Library Association, he held it after hours at the London Library and asked the committee's permission afterwards. When the committee employed Joseph Gostick to help him compile a new catalogue, he very soon had Gostick working on a lucrative school textbook, Gostick and Harrison's *Outlines of German Litera-*

ture, and Jones's carriage arrears book, once filled with the respectful reminiscences of members, was turned into an accounts book for their joint royalties.

It was Harrison's treatment of Jones that in the end got him into trouble. With the stock of books constantly increasing, Harrison was asked to give up two of his private rooms on the top floor to store books. He seemed to welcome this, wanting as he said to move to the country. When he told Bodham Donne that he was being 'forced out by the folios', Bodham Donne had had them both in stitches by saying 'Ah, you want to *exfoliate!*'

The committee also offered him £80 a year compensation. Harrison banked the compensation and continued to use both rooms. It was then, after years of humiliation, that John Edward Jones rose from the depths and struck. He wrote to every member of the committee, denouncing Harrison. Both Bodham Donne and Christie were on Jones's side, and there is alarming evidence of Harrison's rage when roused in the note scored into the arrears book at the time: 'I think W. D. Christie must be a half-breed. He never could have mixed with English gentlemen so long and preserved that vile nature if he were of pure Saxon or Norman descent. A negro or South American Indian would surely be found in his pedigree – if it could be traced, which I doubt.'

Christie, Herbert Spencer and Jones's other supporters did their best, and it would have been a just and happy end if Jones, for even a couple of years, could have been Librarian of the London Library. The Harrison faction on the committee won, not by entirely undevious means. But in a sense justice was done. Douglas Matthews and I only discovered this after the history of the Library had gone to press, but Leslie Stephen was Chairman of the Committee, and Harrison, having wangled his mother and both his obscure brothers into the *Dictionary of National Biography*, was never to appear in it himself.

*

It would, finally, be impossible in the space available to do full justice to the London Library's greatest Librarian, Charles Hagberg Wright.

Hagberg ran the library for nearly fifty years: when he applied for the job in 1892 the principal librarian at the British Museum was being paid £1,200 a year: the salary at St James's Square was £400 with no pension. There were over 250 candidates. Hagberg Wright was unanimously elected.

He found the Library an amateurishly catalogued collection of books overflowing onto the stairs of an old brick town house that was hemmed in on every side by freeholds and ancient lights that effectively prevented its expansion in any direction.

Hagberg, at last, was the general that Carlyle had dreamed of. He planned the Library's expansion westwards towards Duke Street, looking ahead a hundred years and making possible the building work being done today. He inspired the fund-raising, he showed himself a master of public relations in promoting the Library in the newspapers, he engaged Osborne Smith to build the much-loved stacks, transferring books so efficiently that during the entire building work and the demolition of Beauchamp House the Library was only closed for three weeks. Working with Purnell in the little room under the roof, sometimes for eighteen hours a day, he individually examined, marked, recatalogued and rehoused 170,000 books. On the wall he had a typed notice: 'No guessing, no thinking, accuracy, accuracy, accuracy!' It is Hagberg who still leads us from *Ballooning* to *Baths*, from *Bells* to *Betting (see Gambling)*.

He was also, like Cochrane, a bibliomaniac, and friends remembered him on holiday in Rome buying two books, a life of St Elizabeth of Portugal, and *Silica and Kindred Minerals*, and enjoying them both alternately, one page at a time.

By the 1914 War he was a national figure, reading the Russian press for the Government. When a question was asked in the House of Commons about a leak that had appeared in a Russian newspaper from an unknown source, the Home Secretary quoted 'the Librarian of the London Library, Dr Hagberg Wright, *whom everybody knows!*' This was greeted, according to *Hansard*, with cheers and cries of 'Hear Hear!'

At the time he had founded and was running the Red Cross Library, collecting and distributing books to field hospitals, and on his own initiative sending over eight tons of books to Russian prisoners in Germany.

He was an acquaintance, friend and translator of Tolstoy, a close friend of Henry James. Arthur Ransome said that even Hagberg's signature was so impressive that he could get through any roadblock in revolutionary Russia simply by flourishing a letter from the Librarian asking for some overdue books.

After the First War, when he was nearly sixty, he married a bossy widow, Constance Tyrrell Lewis, remembered by one relative of Hagberg's as 'a rather starched-up woman'. A caricature she had drawn, *Snowed Under*, satirising the lack of bookspace, showed Hagberg sitting under a tarpaulin surrounded by heaps of unaccommodated books, was hung on the stairs among all the sidewhiskered Victorian worthies; she also organised fund-raising *At Homes* in the Reading Room, competing in grandeur with Lady Astor's parties at the other side of the Square, the stairs lined with black-uniformed members of the staff, sometimes with an exhibition of rare books, sometimes with folksingers or instrumentalists.

He was not without fault. There is no doubt that Hagberg towards the end of his life had a tendency to 'admire' rare books in country houses where he spent the weekend in the same way the late Queen Mary used to 'admire' valuable antiques. He became obsessive about his building schemes, and I have written at length about his troubles with the Prévost Bequest, when he upset the staff by earmarking for the building fund a house in Kent that had been left specifically to them, and lost a lot of money on unnecessary legal wrangles in Canada.

But his last years were full of honours. He was knighted, the Library recieved its Royal Charter, and he died happy, like a good bibliomaniac, examining a new collection of books for the Library on the subject of the Caucasus.

A few days ago I received a remarkable letter from Armine Charles Almroth Wright, a direct descendent of the Dutch protestant Arminius, and Hagberg's nephew. What he had to tell me was fascinating.

Hagberg's mother and aunt, Ebba and Emma Almroth, daughters of the Keeper of the Royal Mint in Stockholm, enrolled themselves, when their parents died, for an Evangelical conference in Lausanne. There they met and were virtually adopted by a childless Yorkshire clergyman. His wife, Lady Alicia Blackwood, took them as nurses to Scutari, and eventually married them off to her husband's curates, one of them Hagberg's father.

But if he got his Nordic good looks from his Swedish mother, it was his father's side of the family to which he owed his intelligence, and which provides some psychological explanation of his amazing energy and stamina.

His grandfather was a leading Anglo-Irish lawyer. His uncle, Percival Wright, a friend of Charles Darwin, was Secretary of the Royal Irish Academy. A distinguished adademic, he was the author of *The Pathology of the Squint* and an authority on birds, fungi, molluscs, minnows and the blind cave creatures of Ireland.

More alarmingly, his father, Charles Henry Hamilton Wright, was a passionate anti-Catholic, author of *The Pope as Anti-Christ*. He was also one of the first to subject the Old Testament to historical criticism, making him a man of too advanced views for work as a parish priest, and he was sent from his curacy in Yorkshire where Hagberg was born in 1862 to be English Chaplain in Dresden. Hence Hagberg's upbringing abroad. In Dresden he was hounded out by expatriate Anglo-Catholics, outraged further by his sermons against slavery in the United States, and was offered the English chaplaincy at Boulogne sur Mer, where he founded one of the first Missions to Seamen. Even there his work among German prisoners during the Franco-Prussian war and the subsequent gratitude of the Kaiser made him unpopular with the French.

The family returned to Ireland, where Hagberg and his four brothers were sent to the Belfast Academical Institution, teased and bullied for their foreignness. It was this experience, Armine Wright believes, that hardened them and made them so ambitious. They all distinguished themselves at school, and at Trinity College, Dublin.

Armine Wright hints that it may have been some affair of the heart that made the young Hagberg give up his assistant librarianship in Dublin to come to St James's Square, but what must have driven him most of all was a sense of competitiveness with the rest of the family.

His father was still a controversial public figure as a leading light in the Protestant Truth Society, his younger brother Henry had become a general in the Engineers, and the eldest, Eric, father of Armine Wright, was Chief Justice of the Seychelles, which solves the mystery of why unwanted London Library books were always sent to a public library there.

But by far the greatest competition came from the brother to whom he was closest, Almroth, knighted thirty years before Hagberg for services to immunology. He was spoken of in the same breath as Pasteur, and was the first to inoculate himself against typhus after the terrible losses from that disease in the Boer War. He too, was a brilliant public figure, known to have abandoned medicine for a year at Dublin out of boredom with medicine and to have taken up Italian Renaissance literature. But his great passion in life, when Hagberg was rebuilding the London Library, was the Womens' Movement.

His tract, published in 1913, *The Unexpurgated Case Against*

Woman Suffrage – briefly that women go mad once a month – is to be found in *Science* and *Miscellaneous*, according to Hagberg's classification, between *Witchcraft* and *Woollens*.

Men in favour of the vote for women, he says, are either cranks or 'that very curious type of man, who when it is suggested in his hearing that the species woman is, measured by certain intellectual and moral standards, the inferior of the species man, solemnly draws himself up and asks "Are you, Sir, aware that you are insulting my wife?"'

Hardly surprising then, that Hagberg was so driven, and all the more credit to him that he became Librarian of a Library where independent women were from the first so well represented, and where that other Irish terror, Alice Stopford Green, who so terrified General Smuts, served on the committee for the first twenty years of his Librarianship.

Armine Wright, surprisingly enough, found my account of his uncle's troubles with the Prévost Bequest entirely plausible. When Uncle Almroth came to call, he always left 'a layer of half-crowns' for the children. Every penny Hagberg had went to the London Library.

But Armine Wright's most touching memory of 'Uncle Charlie' is of when he came to visit them for Sunday lunch. Afterwards, hymns were played on the piano, and Uncle Charlie would sit 'with the tears pouring down'. With an acrobatic leap to a conclusion even I would hesitate to make, Armine Wright adds: 'I wondered sometimes whether his tears were due to the fact that he could not acknowledge any children he had sired in the most unexpected situations.'

Such giddy speculation apart, an understanding of Hagberg's Anglo-Irish family adds to his heroic stature at the moment I most like to picture him, as a man of thirty-six, his hair parted high on the crown, well-drawn eyebrows arched over rather tender dark eyes, the ends of his moustache waxed, at the opening of the new building with its new stone façade, but occupying the shell of old Beauchamp House, on a winter's afternoon in December 1898.

The Reading Room was stuffy from the unaccustomed crowd of visiting dignitaries, and men identified as members of the Library, by one observant journalist, for their tendency to baldness. He had just made a few jokes, about the kind of questions he was asked as Librarian. 'Who was the Coptic Saint that made a mummy talk in the third century?' 'Had he got a book about a Royal Princess who worked as a cook in London, and made nice curries?' 'Had he got anything about the raising of Lazarus?' To be impartial, he said, he had sent them a Bible and a book on Christian myths.

As he acknowledged the applause of writers, magnates, Members of Parliament, peers, bishops, and even of Sir Garnet Wolseley, the most glamorous soldier in the British Empire at its zenith, as the man who had remade Carlyle's London Library, he must have sensed that, as far as his family was concerned at least, he had finally established his own identity.

A library is not a dead legacy. It is a living organism, and it is the passion and energy of the librarian, as much as its committee and its members, that keeps a library alive.

Cochrane the bibliomaniac, Bodham Donne the dilletante, Harrison the professional, Hagberg Wright who combined all three qualities with those of a driven visionary and politically skilled man of action – each in their way shaped the London Library we are still privileged to possess. I hope Douglas Matthews with his notorious modesty will forgive me if I dedicate this lecture to him in gratitude as their worthy successor.

INDEX